★★★ T H E ★★★

U N I T E D

S T A T E S   O F

A M E R I C A

A State-by-State Guide

MILLIE MILLER AND CYNDI NELSON

★ ★ ★

SCHOLASTIC
REFERENCE

Acknowledgments

Thank you, Ivan and Scott, our enduring husbands and critics.
Tell the kids—Scott, Jon, Tyler, Peter, Jeffrey, and Stina—that we'll be home for dinner.

Special thanks for valuable input to:
Audrey Benedict (Cloud Ridge Naturalists), Brad Easterson (American PIE—Public Information on the Environment), Nancy Laties Feresten (Senior Editor, Scholastic Inc.), Barbara French (Bat Conservation International), Steve Frye and Scott Severs (Boulder Wild Bird Center), Laurie Lanzen Harris (Editor of *Biography Today*, Omnigraphics, Inc.), Boris Kondratieff (Ft. Collins Entomology Department), Chris Pague (The Nature Conservancy), Gerry Roehm (The U.S. Fish and Wildlife Service), Nancy Sabato (Art Director, Scholastic Inc.), Judy Volc (Children's Literature Specialist, Boulder Public Library), Katherine Young and Fran Grzenda (Foothill Elementary Librarians, Boulder, CO), all the folks at Scholastic Inc. who made this project possible, and the many people throughout the U.S.A. who answered our endless questions.

Additional thanks to our support team:
Dr. John Carter (southern gentleman), Ginny Gardner (our Hawaiian connection), Bill and Lyn Gullette (Endaba, Pagosa Springs B&B), Marcy Lockhart (world traveler and teacher), Jake Lucas (resident Montana expert), Carl Mackey (Plant Ecologist, Rocky Mountain Arsenal National Wildlife Refuge), Marilyn Marinelli (educator extraordinaire), Walt and Velma Nelson (grandparents), and Ana Sanjuan (steadfast source of encouragement and nourishment).

Population statistics for the 50 states and Washington, D.C., are estimates for 1998. Puerto Rico's population is an estimate for 1997. All population figures are from the U.S. Bureau of the Census (www.census.gov).

★   ★   ★   ★

LIBRARY OF CONGRESS CATALOGING-IN-PUBLICATION
Miller, Millie. ★ The United States of America: a state-by-state guide. / by Millie Miller and Cyndi Nelson. ★ p.   cm. ★ Includes index. ★ Summary: Presents information about the people, places, birds, insects, flowers, endangered species, and more associated with each of the fifty states and the nation's capital. ★ ISBN 0-590-04374-9 ★ 1.   U.S. states—Miscellanea—Juvenile literature. ★ 2.   U.S. states—Pictorial works—Juvenile literature. ★ [1. United States—Miscellanea.] ★ I. Nelson, Cyndi. ★ II. Title. ★ E180.M55 ★ 1999 ★ 98-40926 ★ 973—dc21 ★ CIP ★ AC

10 9 8 7 6 5 4 3 2   0/0 01 02 03
★ Printed in Mexico   49 ★
Book design by Nancy Sabato
Composition by BNGO Books/Kevin Callahan
First printing, September 1999

Dedicated to the Children of the World

"The survival of
the world depends
upon our sharing what
we have and
working together."

— Frank Fools Crow,
Teton Sioux

The U.S.–Canadian Border is the longest undefended border in the world.

CANADA

WASHINGTON

OREGON

Cascade Mountains

IDAHO

MONTANA

NORTH DAKOTA

Missouri River

WYOMING

Continental Divide

ROCKY

SOUTH DAKOTA

NEBRASKA

Sierra Nevada Mountains

Pacific Ocean

NEVADA

UTAH

Mountains

COLORADO

KANSAS

CALIFORNIA

Colorado River

Death Valley is the lowest spot in the nation, at 282 feet below sea level.

ARIZONA

NEW MEXICO

National bird: Bald eagle

The northernmost point in the U.S.A. is Point Barrow, AK.

TEXAS

MEXICO

Rio Grande

Each year, it rains about 460 inches on the wettest place in the world, Mt. Waialeale, Kauai.

ALASKA

HAWAII

Cape Wrangel, AK, is the westernmost point in the U.S.A.

Denali is the highest mountain in North America. It is 20,320 feet.

Ka Lae, HI, is the southernmost point in the U.S.A.

The United States of America was founded July 4, 1776. • Population: 270,298,524 • Area: 3,675,031 square miles

Lake Superior is the largest freshwater lake in the world.

The St. Lawrence Seaway is the longest canal in the world. It is about 450 miles long.

The easternmost point in the U.S.A. is West Quoddy Head, ME.

CANADA

MINNESOTA

Lake Superior

MICHIGAN

WISCONSIN

Lake Huron

Lake Michigan

MICHIGAN

Lake Ontario

St. Lawrence River

MAINE

VERMONT

NEW HAMPSHIRE

MASSACHUSETTS

NEW YORK

RHODE ISLAND

CONNECTICUT

IOWA

ILLINOIS

INDIANA

OHIO

Lake Erie

PENNSYLVANIA

NEW JERSEY

Missouri River

Mississippi River

Ohio River

WEST VIRGINIA

Appalachian Mountains

DELAWARE

MARYLAND

WASHINGTON, D.C.

VIRGINIA

MISSOURI

KENTUCKY

NORTH CAROLINA

OKLAHOMA

ARKANSAS

TENNESSEE

SOUTH CAROLINA

MISSISSIPPI

ALABAMA

GEORGIA

Atlantic Ocean

Extinct: Carolina parakeet. Over 250 U.S. plants and animals have disappeared since 1980.

LOUISIANA

FLORIDA

The Mississippi River is 2,348 miles long. It is the longest river in North America.

Gulf of Mexico

National flower: Rose

Puerto Rico is a U.S. commonwealth and located about 1,000 miles southeast of Miami.

PUERTO RICO

THE UNITED STATES OF AMERICA

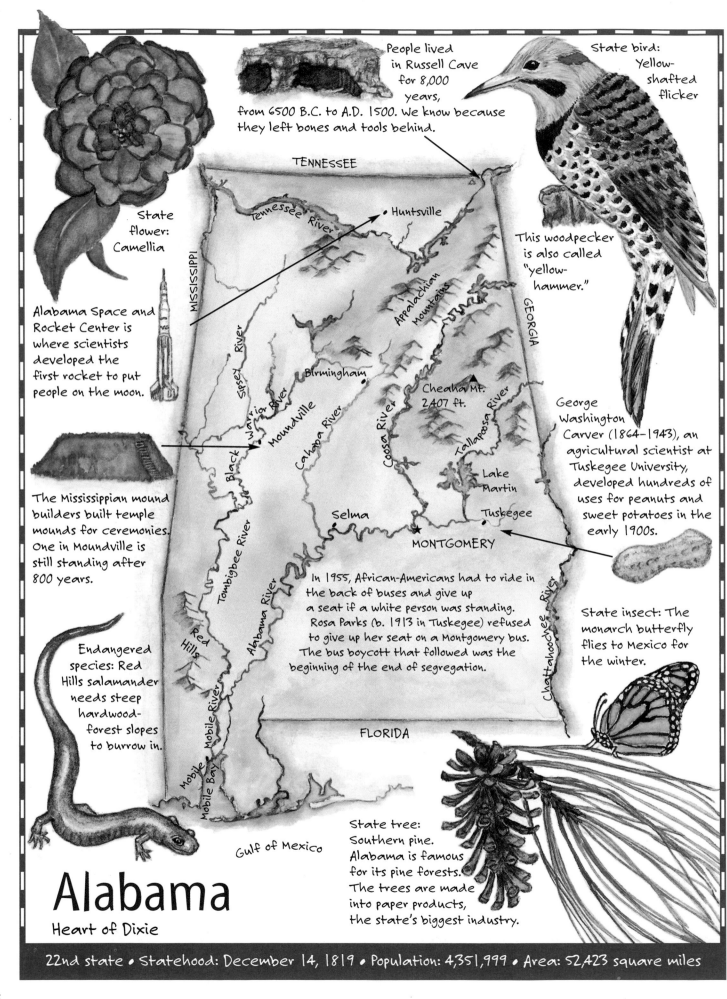

People lived in Russell Cave for 8,000 years, from 6500 B.C. to A.D. 1500. We know because they left bones and tools behind.

State bird: Yellow-shafted flicker

This woodpecker is also called "yellow-hammer."

State flower: Camellia

Alabama Space and Rocket Center is where scientists developed the first rocket to put people on the moon.

The Mississippian mound builders built temple mounds for ceremonies. One in Moundville is still standing after 800 years.

George Washington Carver (1864–1943), an agricultural scientist at Tuskegee University, developed hundreds of uses for peanuts and sweet potatoes in the early 1900s.

In 1955, African-Americans had to ride in the back of buses and give up a seat if a white person was standing. Rosa Parks (b. 1913 in Tuskegee) refused to give up her seat on a Montgomery bus. The bus boycott that followed was the beginning of the end of segregation.

State insect: The monarch butterfly flies to Mexico for the winter.

Endangered species: Red Hills salamander needs steep hardwood-forest slopes to burrow in.

State tree: Southern pine. Alabama is famous for its pine forests. The trees are made into paper products, the state's biggest industry.

TENNESSEE

MISSISSIPPI

GEORGIA

FLORIDA

Tennessee River

Huntsville

Appalachian Mountains

Sipsey River

Black Warrior River

Moundville

Birmingham

Cahaba River

Cheaha Mt. 2,407 ft.

Coosa River

Tallapoosa River

Lake Martin

Tuskegee

Selma

MONTGOMERY

Tombigbee River

Red Hills

Alabama River

Chattahoochee River

Mobile River

Mobile

Mobile Bay

Gulf of Mexico

Alabama

Heart of Dixie

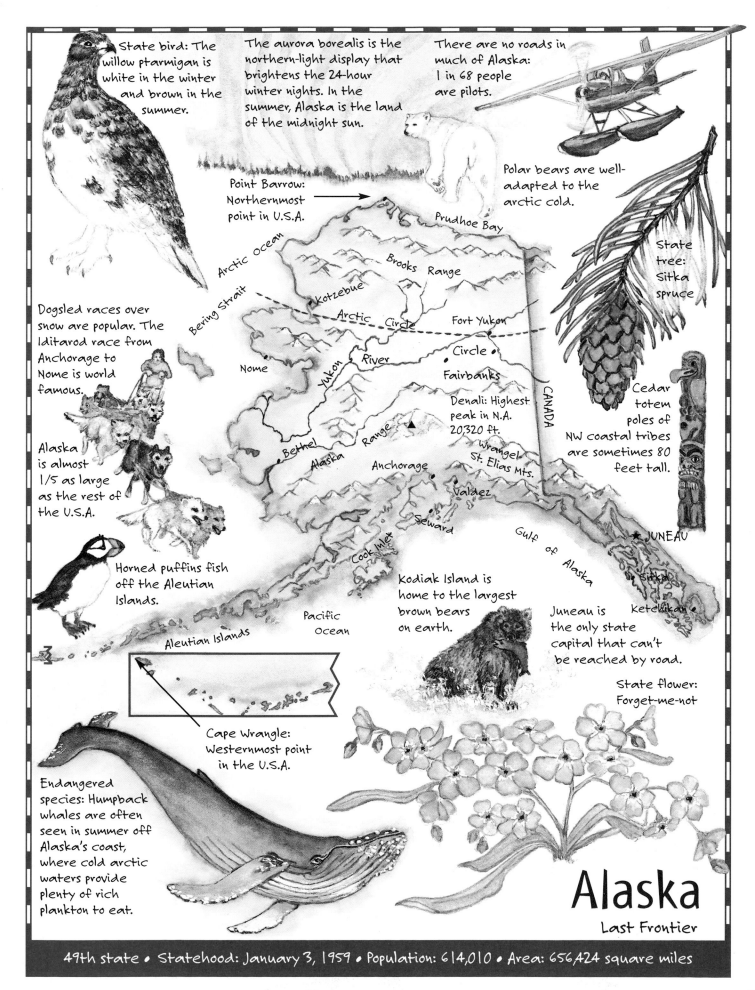

State bird: The willow ptarmigan is white in the winter and brown in the summer.

The aurora borealis is the northern-light display that brightens the 24-hour winter nights. In the summer, Alaska is the land of the midnight sun.

There are no roads in much of Alaska: 1 in 68 people are pilots.

Polar bears are well-adapted to the arctic cold.

Point Barrow: Northernmost point in U.S.A.

Prudhoe Bay

Arctic Ocean

Brooks Range

Kotzebue

State tree: Sitka spruce

Dogsled races over snow are popular. The Iditarod race from Anchorage to Nome is world famous.

Bering Strait

Arctic Circle

Fort Yukon

Nome

Yukon River

Circle

Fairbanks

Denali: Highest peak in N.A. 20,320 ft.

CANADA

Cedar totem poles of NW coastal tribes are sometimes 80 feet tall.

Alaska is almost 1/5 as large as the rest of the U.S.A.

Bethel

Alaska Range

Anchorage

Wrangel St. Elias Mts.

Valdez

Seward

Cook Inlet

Gulf of Alaska

JUNEAU

Sitka

Horned puffins fish off the Aleutian Islands.

Aleutian Islands

Pacific Ocean

Kodiak Island is home to the largest brown bears on earth.

Ketchikan

Juneau is the only state capital that can't be reached by road.

Cape Wrangle: Westernmost point in the U.S.A.

State flower: Forget-me-not

Endangered species: Humpback whales are often seen in summer off Alaska's coast, where cold arctic waters provide plenty of rich plankton to eat.

Alaska
Last Frontier

49th state • Statehood: January 3, 1959 • Population: 614,010 • Area: 656,424 square miles

Endangered species: Sandborn's lesser longnosed bat is a vital part of the nighttime pollination of the saguaro cactus.

The Grand Canyon is a scenic 277-mile-long gorge, one mile deep in some places.

State tree: Paloverde

Canyon de Chelly was home to prehistoric Pueblo Indians.

UTAH

COLORADO

NEVADA

Colorado Plateau

Four Corners

Colorado River

Lake Mead

Humphrey's Peak 12,633 ft.

Painted Desert

Little Colorado River

Petrified Forest

Flagstaff

NEW MEXICO

Hoover Dam regulates the flow of the Colorado River. Its huge generators use the energy of the moving water to make electricity.

CALIFORNIA

Colorado River

Magollon Rim

State flower: Blossoms of the saguaro cactus, the largest cactus in the U.S.A., bloom at night in the Sonoran Desert.

PHOENIX Scottsdale

Tempe

Salt River

Gila River

Gila River

Yuma

Sonoran Desert

Santa Cruz River

Tucson

Kitt Peak National Observatory

Tombstone

Skeleton Canyon

MEXICO

The Tucson area is called the Astronomy Capital of the world because of good star viewing away from city lights and pollution.

Tombstone was a boomtown of the Old West known for gunfights and a cemetery called Boot Hill.

RIP

Geronimo (1829-1909) was a legendary Apache leader. In 1886, his tribe was one of the last to surrender to U.S. troops (in Skeleton Canyon).

State bird: The cactus wren builds a football-shaped nest in several kinds of cactus.

Arizona
Grand Canyon State

48th state • Statehood: February 14, 1912 • Population: 4,668,631 • Area: 114,006 square miles

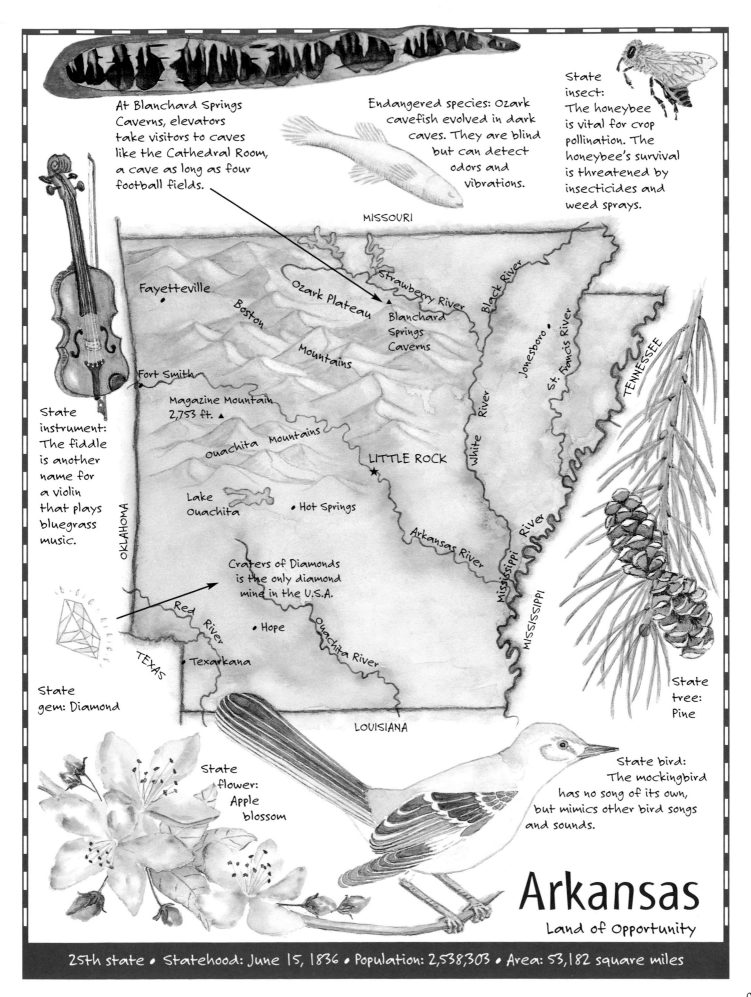

At Blanchard Springs Caverns, elevators take visitors to caves like the Cathedral Room, a cave as long as four football fields.

Endangered species: Ozark cavefish evolved in dark caves. They are blind but can detect odors and vibrations.

State insect: The honeybee is vital for crop pollination. The honeybee's survival is threatened by insecticides and weed sprays.

State instrument: The fiddle is another name for a violin that plays bluegrass music.

State gem: Diamond

MISSOURI

Fayetteville

Ozark Plateau

Strawberry River

Black River

Blanchard Springs Caverns

Jonesboro

St. Francis River

TENNESSEE

Boston Mountains

Fort Smith

Magazine Mountain 2,753 ft. ▲

Ouachita Mountains

White River

LITTLE ROCK

Lake Ouachita

Hot Springs

Craters of Diamonds is the only diamond mine in the U.S.A.

Arkansas River

Mississippi River

OKLAHOMA

Red River

Hope

Ouachita River

MISSISSIPPI

TEXAS

Texarkana

LOUISIANA

State tree: Pine

State flower: Apple blossom

State bird: The mockingbird has no song of its own, but mimics other bird songs and sounds.

Arkansas
Land of Opportunity

25th state • Statehood: June 15, 1836 • Population: 2,538,303 • Area: 53,182 square miles

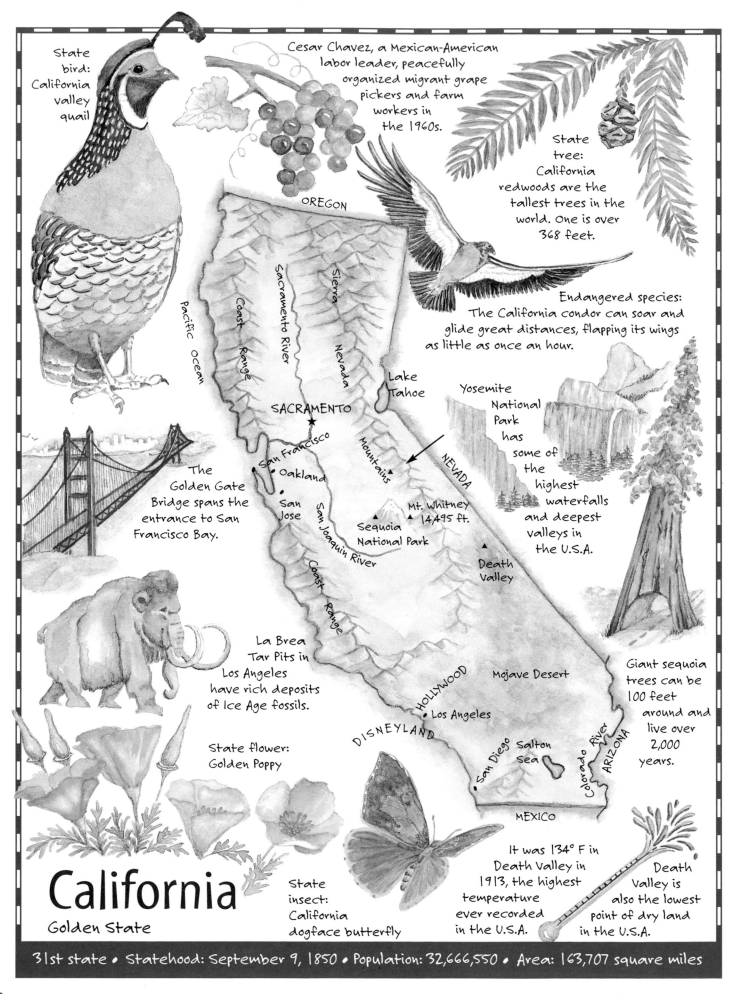

State bird: California valley quail

Cesar Chavez, a Mexican-American labor leader, peacefully organized migrant grape pickers and farm workers in the 1960s.

State tree: California redwoods are the tallest trees in the world. One is over 368 feet.

Endangered species: The California condor can soar and glide great distances, flapping its wings as little as once an hour.

OREGON

Sierra Nevada

Sacramento River

Coast Range

Pacific Ocean

SACRAMENTO

Lake Tahoe

Yosemite National Park has some of the highest waterfalls and deepest valleys in the U.S.A.

The Golden Gate Bridge spans the entrance to San Francisco Bay.

San Francisco
Oakland
San Jose

San Joaquin River

Mountains

NEVADA

Mt. Whitney 14,495 ft.

Sequoia National Park

Death Valley

La Brea Tar Pits in Los Angeles have rich deposits of Ice Age fossils.

Coast Range

Giant sequoia trees can be 100 feet around and live over 2,000 years.

State flower: Golden Poppy

HOLLYWOOD
Los Angeles

DISNEYLAND

Mojave Desert

San Diego
Salton Sea

Colorado River

ARIZONA

MEXICO

California
Golden State

State insect: California dogface butterfly

It was 134° F in Death Valley in 1913, the highest temperature ever recorded in the U.S.A.

Death Valley is also the lowest point of dry land in the U.S.A.

31st state • Statehood: September 9, 1850 • Population: 32,666,550 • Area: 163,707 square miles

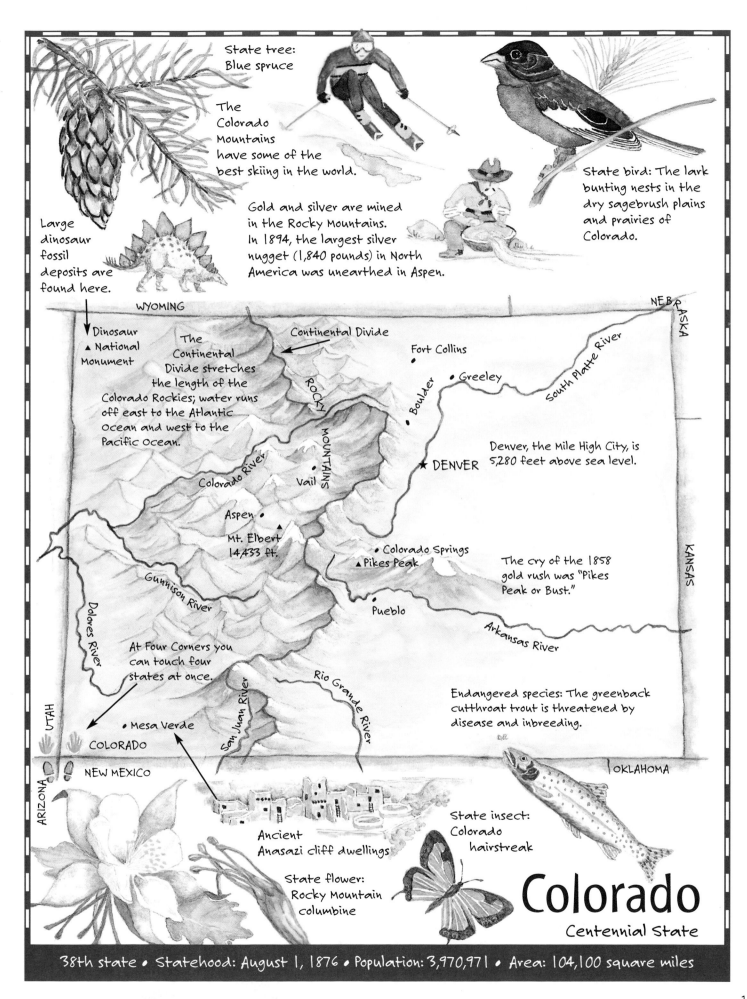

State tree: Blue spruce

The Colorado Mountains have some of the best skiing in the world.

Gold and silver are mined in the Rocky Mountains. In 1894, the largest silver nugget (1,840 pounds) in North America was unearthed in Aspen.

State bird: The lark bunting nests in the dry sagebrush plains and prairies of Colorado.

Large dinosaur fossil deposits are found here.

WYOMING

Dinosaur National Monument

The Continental Divide stretches the length of the Colorado Rockies; water runs off east to the Atlantic Ocean and west to the Pacific Ocean.

Continental Divide

Fort Collins

Greeley

Boulder

ROCKY MOUNTAINS

NEBRASKA

South Platte River

Colorado River

Vail

DENVER

Denver, the Mile High City, is 5,280 feet above sea level.

Aspen

Mt. Elbert 14,433 ft.

Colorado Springs

Pikes Peak

The cry of the 1858 gold rush was "Pikes Peak or Bust."

Gunnison River

Pueblo

KANSAS

Dolores River

At Four Corners you can touch four states at once.

San Juan River

Rio Grande River

Arkansas River

Endangered species: The greenback cutthroat trout is threatened by disease and inbreeding.

UTAH

Mesa Verde

COLORADO

NEW MEXICO

ARIZONA

OKLAHOMA

Ancient Anasazi cliff dwellings

State flower: Rocky Mountain columbine

State insect: Colorado hairstreak

Colorado
Centennial State

38th state • Statehood: August 1, 1876 • Population: 3,970,971 • Area: 104,100 square miles

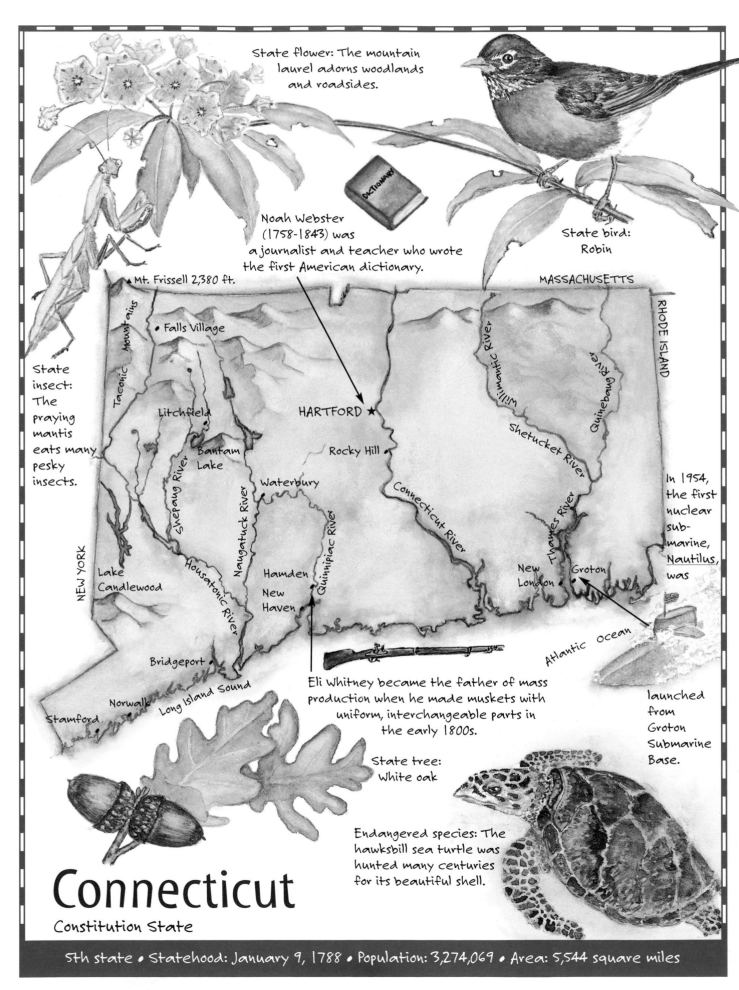

State flower: The mountain laurel adorns woodlands and roadsides.

State bird: Robin

Noah Webster (1758-1843) was a journalist and teacher who wrote the first American dictionary.

State insect: The praying mantis eats many pesky insects.

▲ Mt. Frissell 2,380 ft.

MASSACHUSETTS

RHODE ISLAND

Taconic Mountains

• Falls Village

Litchfield

Bantam Lake

Shepaug River

Naugatuck River

Housatonic River

Waterbury

Quinnipiac River

HARTFORD ★

Rocky Hill •

Connecticut River

Willimantic River

Shetucket River

Quinebaug River

Thames River

New London •

Groton •

NEW YORK

Lake Candlewood

Hamden

New Haven •

Bridgeport •

Norwalk •

Long Island Sound

Stamford •

Atlantic Ocean

In 1954, the first nuclear submarine, Nautilus, was launched from Groton Submarine Base.

Eli Whitney became the father of mass production when he made muskets with uniform, interchangeable parts in the early 1800s.

State tree: White oak

Endangered species: The hawksbill sea turtle was hunted many centuries for its beautiful shell.

Connecticut
Constitution State

5th state • Statehood: January 9, 1788 • Population: 3,274,069 • Area: 5,544 square miles

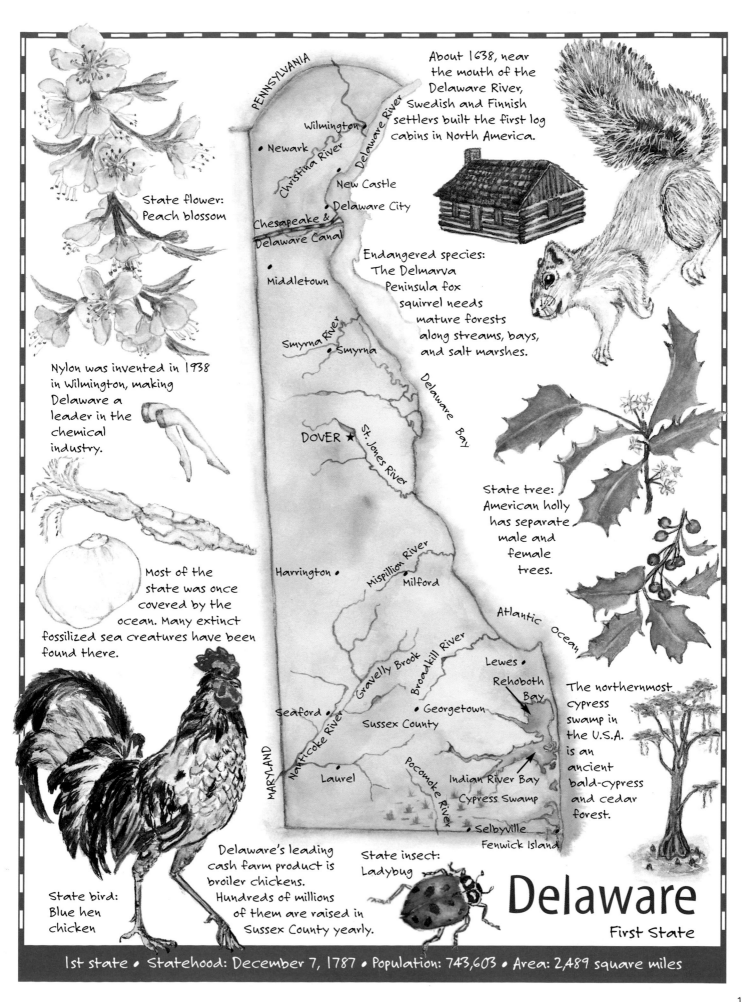

State flower: Peach blossom

Nylon was invented in 1938 in Wilmington, making Delaware a leader in the chemical industry.

Most of the state was once covered by the ocean. Many extinct fossilized sea creatures have been found there.

State bird: Blue hen chicken

PENNSYLVANIA

Wilmington
• Newark
Christina River
Delaware River
New Castle
• Delaware City
Chesapeake & Delaware Canal
• Middletown

Smyrna River
• Smyrna

DOVER ★
St. Jones River

Harrington •
Mispillion River
Milford

Gravelly Brook
Broadkill River
Seaford •
Nanticoke River
Georgetown •
Sussex County
Lewes •
Rehoboth Bay

• Laurel
Pocomoke River
Indian River Bay
Cypress Swamp
• Selbyville
Fenwick Island

MARYLAND

Delaware Bay

Atlantic Ocean

About 1638, near the mouth of the Delaware River, Swedish and Finnish settlers built the first log cabins in North America.

Endangered species: The Delmarva Peninsula fox squirrel needs mature forests along streams, bays, and salt marshes.

State tree: American holly has separate male and female trees.

The northernmost cypress swamp in the U.S.A. is an ancient bald-cypress and cedar forest.

Delaware's leading cash farm product is broiler chickens. Hundreds of millions of them are raised in Sussex County yearly.

State insect: Ladybug

Delaware
First State

State insect: Giant swallowtail butterfly

State flower: Orange blossom

State bird: Mockingbird

Florida grows 80% of the nation's oranges and grapefruits.

ALABAMA

Perdido River

• Pensacola

GEORGIA

Apalachicola River

★ TALLAHASSEE

Gulf of Mexico

Apalachicola

Suwannee River

St. Mary's River

Jacksonville •

St. John's River

The oldest European settlement in North America was founded at St. Augustine in 1565.

Gainesville •

Lake George

Daytona Beach

Pensacola Naval Air Station is home to the Blue Angels, the Navy's famous aerobatic team.

Near Orlando are Epcot Center and Walt Disney World.

Orlando

Kissimmee

Cape Canaveral launches the space shuttle.

State tree: Sabal palm

Florida has more "champions," or largest living tree specimens, than any other state.

• Tampa
• St. Petersburg

Tampa Bay

• Sarasota

Lake Okeechobee

Florida waters have more kinds of fish than any other place in the world.

Wild flamingos are now extinct in Florida.

Captiva Island

Sanibel Island

Florida Keys—150-mile chain of small islands, connected by highway.

Ft. Lauderdale •

The Everglades

Miami •

Atlantic Ocean

Key Largo

Endangered species: The Florida manatee, a gentle "sea cow," cannot swim fast enough to avoid boat propellers near coasts.

Key West

Sunken treasures found here.

Florida
Sunshine State

27th state • Statehood: March 3, 1845 • Population: 14,915,980 • Area: 65,756 square miles

14

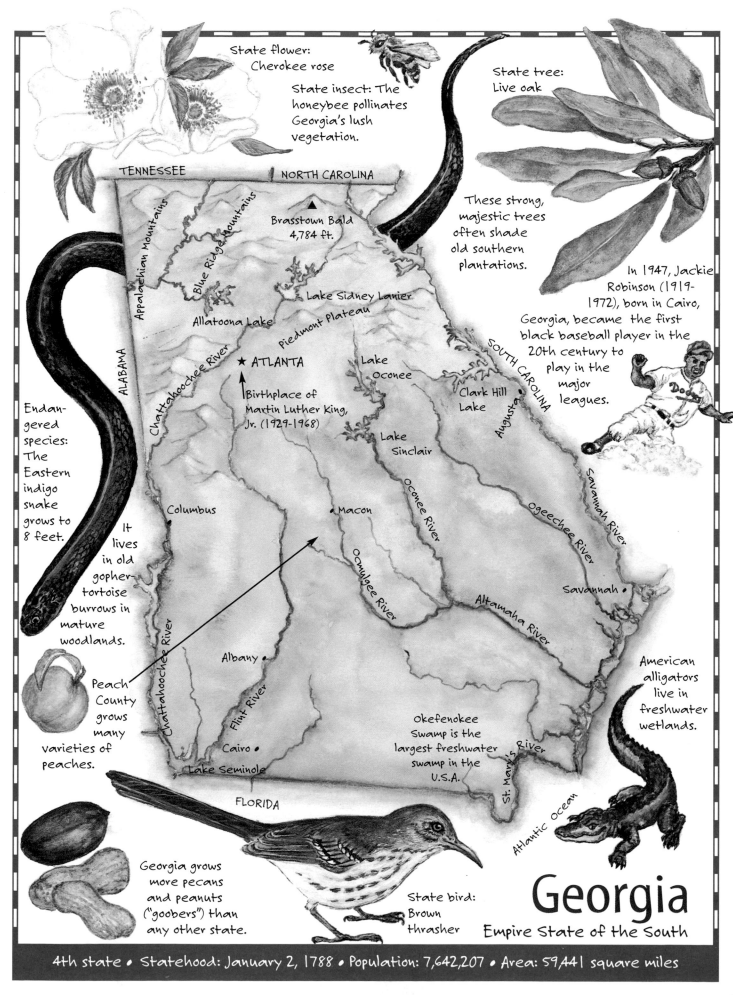

State flower: Cherokee rose

State insect: The honeybee pollinates Georgia's lush vegetation.

State tree: Live oak

These strong, majestic trees often shade old southern plantations.

In 1947, Jackie Robinson (1919-1972), born in Cairo, Georgia, became the first black baseball player in the 20th century to play in the major leagues.

TENNESSEE
NORTH CAROLINA
SOUTH CAROLINA
ALABAMA
FLORIDA

Appalachian Mountains
Blue Ridge Mountains
Brasstown Bald 4,784 ft.
Lake Sidney Lanier
Allatoona Lake
Piedmont Plateau
Chattahoochee River
★ ATLANTA
Birthplace of Martin Luther King, Jr. (1929-1968)
Lake Oconee
Clark Hill Lake
Augusta
Lake Sinclair
Oconee River
Columbus
Macon
Ogeechee River
Savannah River
Savannah
Ocmulgee River
Altamaha River
Albany
Flint River
Chattahoochee River
Cairo
Lake Seminole
Okefenokee Swamp is the largest freshwater swamp in the U.S.A.
St. Mary's River
Atlantic Ocean

Endangered species: The Eastern indigo snake grows to 8 feet. It lives in old gopher-tortoise burrows in mature woodlands.

Peach County grows many varieties of peaches.

American alligators live in freshwater wetlands.

Georgia grows more pecans and peanuts ("goobers") than any other state.

State bird: Brown thrasher

Georgia
Empire State of the South

The Hawaiian alphabet has 12 letters: AEHIKLMNOPUW. "Aloha" means both "hello" and "good-bye."

This mountain is the wettest place on earth. It has an average annual rainfall of 460 inches.

NIIHAU

KAUAI
▲ Mt. Waialeale

State flower: Yellow hibiscus

Pacific Ocean

Hula means "dance" in Hawaiian. Each dance tells a story.

State tree: Kukui tree

The Hawaiian Islands were formed by volcanoes. Some are still active.

OAHU

Pearl Harbor

HONOLULU ★   Kailua

Pacific Ocean

MOLOKAI

Whales winter in Hawaii's warm waters.

LANAI

Home of the largest pineapple plantation in the world.

Lahaina

MAUI

KAHOOLAWE

Haleakala Crater

State bird: The Nene, an island goose, is now rare.

Mauna Kea 13,796 ft. ▲

Hilo

HAWAII

Pacific Ocean

Surfing, the oldest sport in the U.S.A., started in Hawaii long before Columbus sailed.

Queen Liliuokalani (1838-1917) was the last of Hawaii's royalty to live in the only palace in the U.S.A.

▲ Ka Lae: southernmost point in the U.S.A.

Endangered species: Hawaiian monk seals find a safe home in an island wildlife refuge.

Hawaii
Aloha State

50th state • Statehood: August 21, 1959 • Population: 1,193,001 • Area: 10,932 square miles

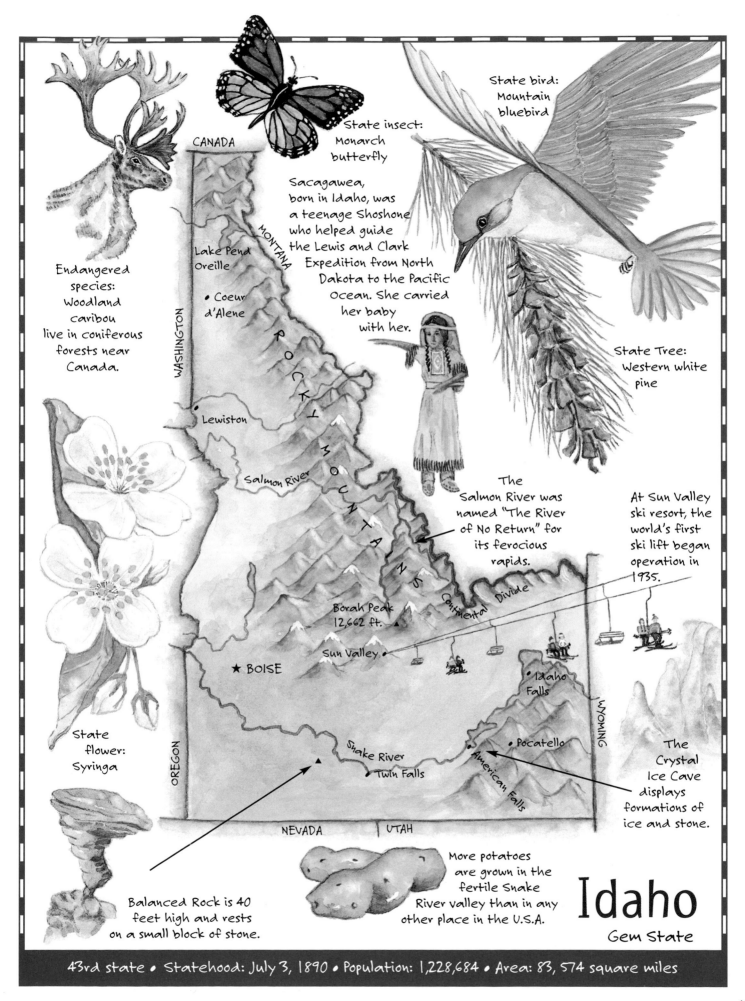

State bird:
Mountain
bluebird

State insect:
Monarch
butterfly

Sacagawea,
born in Idaho, was
a teenage Shoshone
who helped guide
the Lewis and Clark
Expedition from North
Dakota to the Pacific
Ocean. She carried
her baby
with her.

Endangered
species:
Woodland
caribou
live in coniferous
forests near
Canada.

CANADA

MONTANA

Lake Pend
Oreille

WASHINGTON

• Coeur
d'Alene

R O C K Y

• Lewiston

M O U N T A I N S

Salmon River

State Tree:
Western white
pine

The
Salmon River was
named "The River
of No Return" for
its ferocious
rapids.

At Sun Valley
ski resort, the
world's first
ski lift began
operation in
1935.

Borah Peak
12,662 ft. ▲

Continental Divide

Sun Valley •

★ BOISE

OREGON

State
flower:
Syringa

Balanced Rock is 40
feet high and rests
on a small block of stone.

Snake River
• Twin Falls

NEVADA | UTAH

• Idaho
Falls

• Pocatello

American Falls

WYOMING

The
Crystal
Ice Cave
displays
formations of
ice and stone.

More potatoes
are grown in the
fertile Snake
River valley than in any
other place in the U.S.A.

Idaho
Gem State

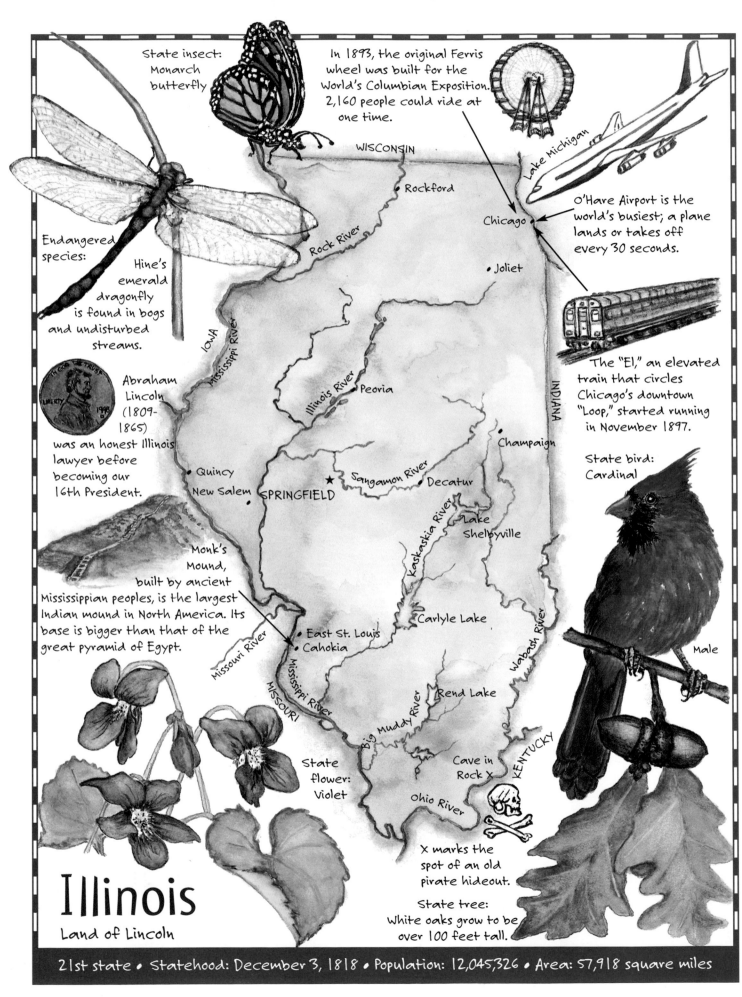

State insect: Monarch butterfly

In 1893, the original Ferris wheel was built for the World's Columbian Exposition. 2,160 people could ride at one time.

Endangered species: Hine's emerald dragonfly is found in bogs and undisturbed streams.

Abraham Lincoln (1809-1865) was an honest Illinois lawyer before becoming our 16th President.

Monk's Mound, built by ancient Mississippian peoples, is the largest Indian mound in North America. Its base is bigger than that of the great pyramid of Egypt.

O'Hare Airport is the world's busiest; a plane lands or takes off every 30 seconds.

The "El," an elevated train that circles Chicago's downtown "Loop," started running in November 1897.

State bird: Cardinal

Male

State flower: Violet

X marks the spot of an old pirate hideout.

State tree: White oaks grow to be over 100 feet tall.

WISCONSIN

Rockford

Lake Michigan

Chicago

Joliet

IOWA

Rock River

Mississippi River

Illinois River

Peoria

INDIANA

Champaign

Quincy

New Salem

SPRINGFIELD

Sangamon River

Decatur

Kaskaskia River

Lake Shelbyville

Carlyle Lake

Wabash River

Missouri River

East St. Louis

Cahokia

Mississippi River

MISSOURI

Rend Lake

Big Muddy River

Cave in Rock X

KENTUCKY

Ohio River

Illinois
Land of Lincoln

21st state • Statehood: December 3, 1818 • Population: 12,045,326 • Area: 57,918 square miles

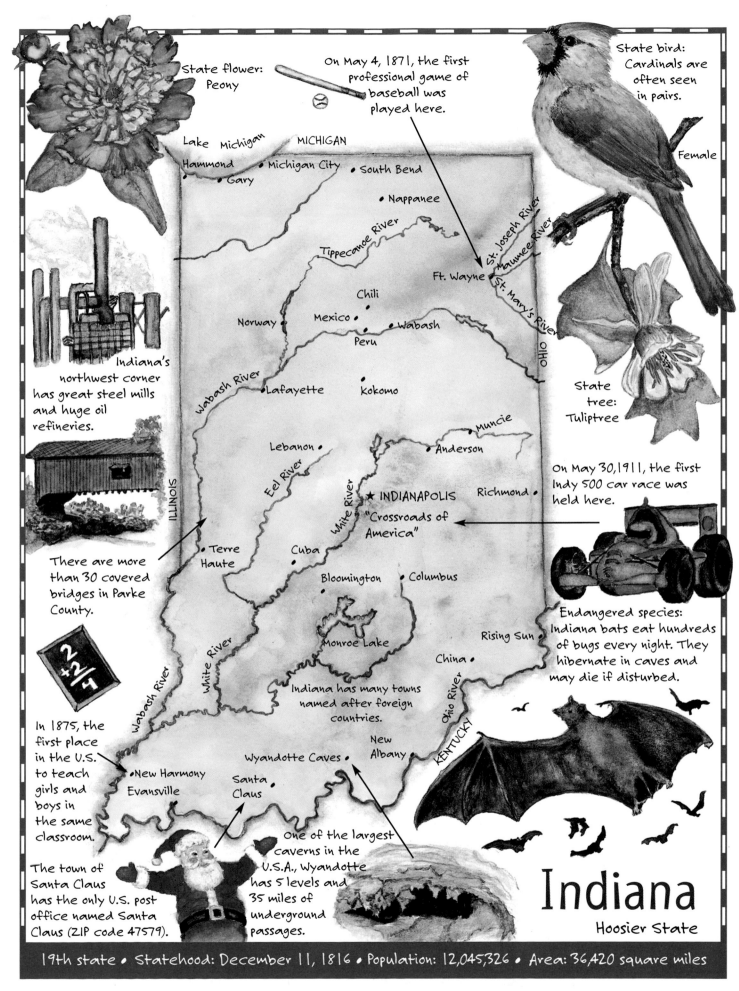

State flower: Peony

On May 4, 1871, the first professional game of baseball was played here.

State bird: Cardinals are often seen in pairs.

Female

Lake Michigan

MICHIGAN

Hammond
Gary
Michigan City
South Bend
Nappanee

Tippecanoe River

St. Joseph River
Maumee River
Ft. Wayne
St. Mary's River
OHIO

Chili
Norway
Mexico
Peru
Wabash

Indiana's northwest corner has great steel mills and huge oil refineries.

Wabash River
Lafayette
Kokomo

State tree: Tuliptree

Muncie
Lebanon
Anderson

There are more than 30 covered bridges in Parke County.

ILLINOIS

Eel River
White River

★ INDIANAPOLIS
"Crossroads of America"

Richmond

On May 30, 1911, the first Indy 500 car race was held here.

Terre Haute
Cuba

Bloomington
Columbus

Endangered species: Indiana bats eat hundreds of bugs every night. They hibernate in caves and may die if disturbed.

White River

Monroe Lake

Rising Sun

China

Indiana has many towns named after foreign countries.

Wabash River

Ohio River

KENTUCKY

In 1875, the first place in the U.S. to teach girls and boys in the same classroom.

New Harmony
Evansville

Wyandotte Caves

Santa Claus

New Albany

The town of Santa Claus has the only U.S. post office named Santa Claus (ZIP code 47579).

One of the largest caverns in the U.S.A., Wyandotte has 5 levels and 35 miles of underground passages.

Indiana
Hoosier State

19th state • Statehood: December 11, 1816 • Population: 12,045,326 • Area: 36,420 square miles

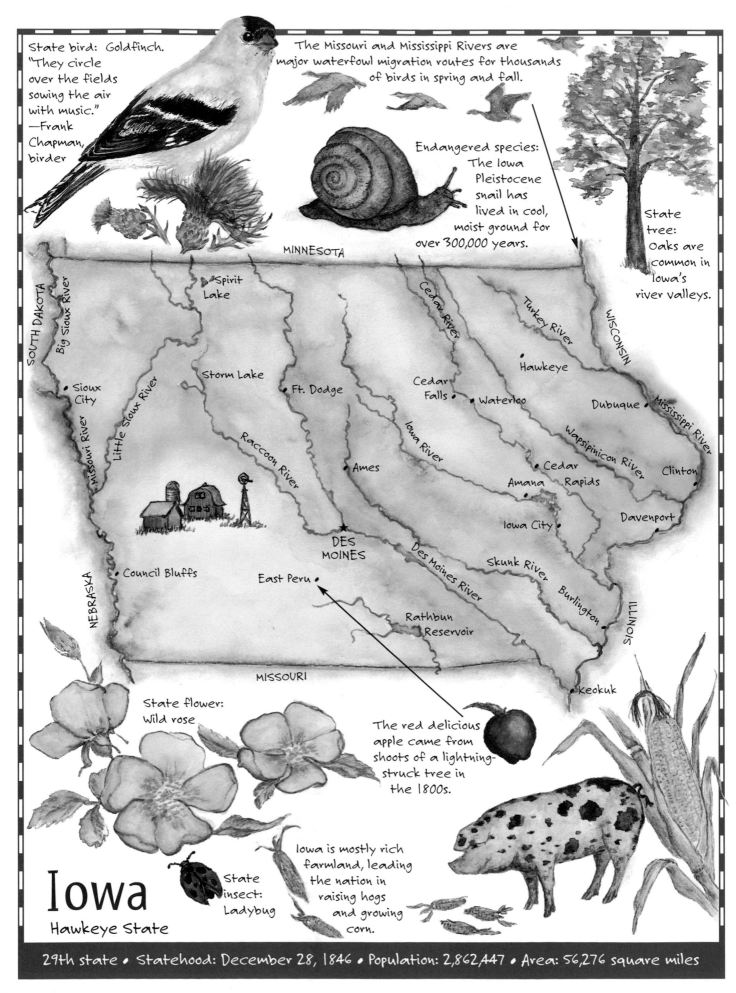

State bird: Goldfinch. "They circle over the fields sowing the air with music." —Frank Chapman, birder

The Missouri and Mississippi Rivers are major waterfowl migration routes for thousands of birds in spring and fall.

Endangered species: The Iowa Pleistocene snail has lived in cool, moist ground for over 300,000 years.

State tree: Oaks are common in Iowa's river valleys.

MINNESOTA

SOUTH DAKOTA

Big Sioux River

Spirit Lake

Cedar River

Turkey River

WISCONSIN

Sioux City

Little Sioux River

Storm Lake

Ft. Dodge

Cedar Falls

Hawkeye

Waterloo

Dubuque

Mississippi River

Missouri River

Raccoon River

Iowa River

Wapsipinicon River

Clinton

Ames

Amana

Cedar Rapids

Davenport

Iowa City

DES MOINES

Council Bluffs

East Peru

Des Moines River

Skunk River

Burlington

ILLINOIS

NEBRASKA

Rathbun Reservoir

MISSOURI

Keokuk

State flower: Wild rose

The red delicious apple came from shoots of a lightning-struck tree in the 1800s.

Iowa
Hawkeye State

State insect: Ladybug

Iowa is mostly rich farmland, leading the nation in raising hogs and growing corn.

29th state • Statehood: December 28, 1846 • Population: 2,862,447 • Area: 56,276 square miles

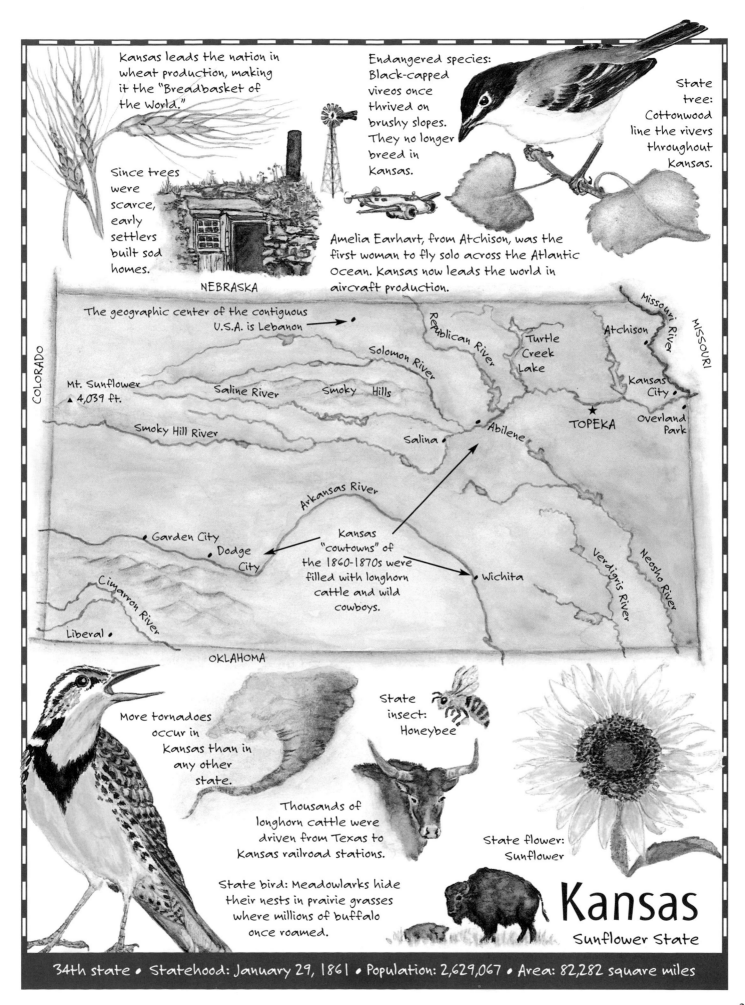

Kansas leads the nation in wheat production, making it the "Breadbasket of the World."

Since trees were scarce, early settlers built sod homes.

Endangered species: Black-capped vireos once thrived on brushy slopes. They no longer breed in Kansas.

State tree: Cottonwood line the rivers throughout Kansas.

Amelia Earhart, from Atchison, was the first woman to fly solo across the Atlantic Ocean. Kansas now leads the world in aircraft production.

NEBRASKA

COLORADO

The geographic center of the contiguous U.S.A. is Lebanon

Republican River

Solomon River

Turtle Creek Lake

Missouri River

MISSOURI

Atchison

Mt. Sunflower ▲ 4,039 ft.

Saline River

Smoky Hills

Kansas City

Smoky Hill River

Salina

Abilene

TOPEKA

Overland Park

Arkansas River

Garden City

Dodge City

Kansas "cowtowns" of the 1860-1870s were filled with longhorn cattle and wild cowboys.

Wichita

Verdigris River

Neosho River

Cimarron River

Liberal

OKLAHOMA

More tornadoes occur in Kansas than in any other state.

State insect: Honeybee

Thousands of longhorn cattle were driven from Texas to Kansas railroad stations.

State flower: Sunflower

State bird: Meadowlarks hide their nests in prairie grasses where millions of buffalo once roamed.

Kansas
Sunflower State

34th state • Statehood: January 29, 1861 • Population: 2,629,067 • Area: 82,282 square miles

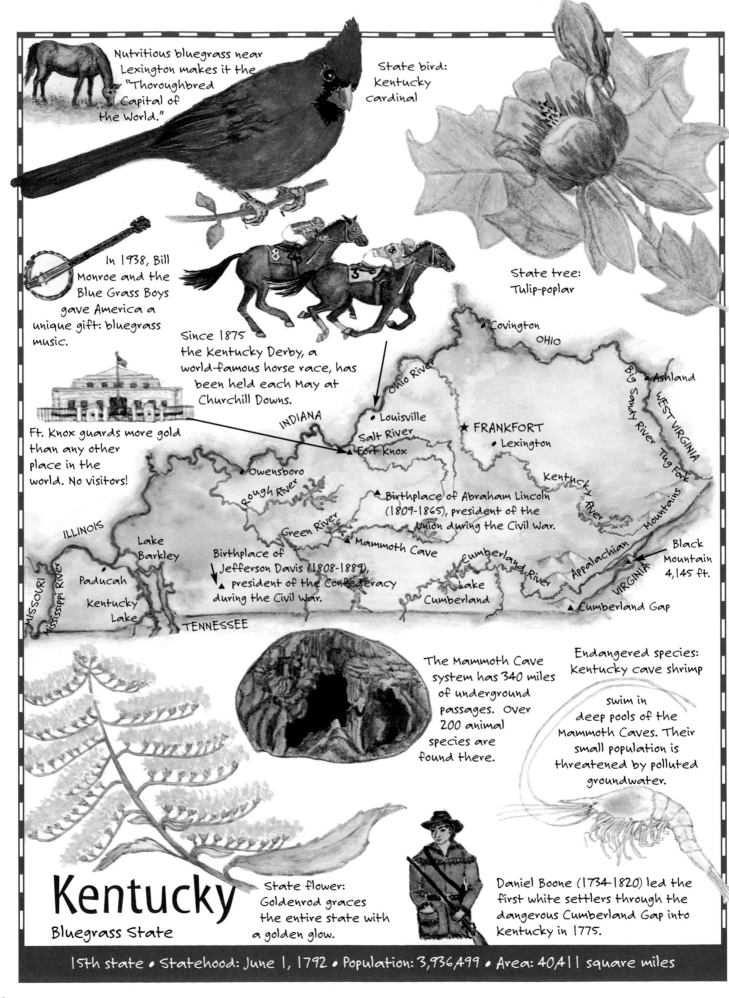

Nutritious bluegrass near Lexington makes it the "Thoroughbred Capital of the World."

State bird: Kentucky cardinal

State tree: Tulip-poplar

In 1938, Bill Monroe and the Blue Grass Boys gave America a unique gift: bluegrass music.

Since 1875 the Kentucky Derby, a world-famous horse race, has been held each May at Churchill Downs.

Ft. Knox guards more gold than any other place in the world. No visitors!

Covington
OHIO
Ohio River
Big Sandy River Tug Fork
Ashland
WEST VIRGINIA
INDIANA
• Louisville
Salt River
Fort Knox
★ FRANKFORT
• Lexington
Kentucky River
• Owensboro
Rough River
▲ Birthplace of Abraham Lincoln (1809-1865), president of the Union during the Civil War.
ILLINOIS
Lake Barkley
Green River
▲ Mammoth Cave
Appalachian Mountains
Black Mountain 4,145 ft.
MISSOURI
Mississippi River
Paducah
Kentucky Lake
Birthplace of Jefferson Davis (1808-1889), president of the Confederacy during the Civil War.
Cumberland River
Lake Cumberland
VIRGINIA
▲ Cumberland Gap
TENNESSEE

The Mammoth Cave system has 340 miles of underground passages. Over 200 animal species are found there.

Endangered species: Kentucky cave shrimp swim in deep pools of the Mammoth Caves. Their small population is threatened by polluted groundwater.

Kentucky
Bluegrass State

State flower: Goldenrod graces the entire state with a golden glow.

Daniel Boone (1734-1820) led the first white settlers through the dangerous Cumberland Gap into Kentucky in 1775.

15th state • Statehood: June 1, 1792 • Population: 3,936,499 • Area: 40,411 square miles

State flower:
Magnolia blossom

Endangered species: Louisiana black bear

State tree:
Baldcypress

It hides in the dense underbrush of hardwood forests.

ARKANSAS

Shreveport

Driskill Mt. 535 ft.

Monroe

Ouachita River

Red River

Mississippi River

TEXAS

Alexandria

Spanish moss hangs from cypress and oak trees in bayous. Bayous are slow-moving streams in or out of swamps, lakes, or the ocean.

MISSISSIPPI

Pearl River

Mardi Gras is a holiday celebrated with parades, parties, feasts, and costume balls. Everyone wears a mask.

Sabine River

Bayou Boeuf

Bayou Teche

Atchafalaya River

Bayou Nezpique

Calcasieu River

State insect: Honeybee

Lafayette

Lake Pontchartrain

★ BATON ROUGE

Birthplace of jazz and Louis (Satchmo) Armstrong (1900?–1971), world renowned for his trumpet sounds.

Sabine Lake

Calcasieu Lake

Lake Charles

Grand Lake

Avery Island

White Lake

New Orleans

Bayou Lafourche

Thousands of egrets, herons, and other birds flock to Avery Island and the swampy woods for safety.

Gulf of Mexico

The world's largest indoor arena, the Louisiana Superdome in New Orleans, has 95,427 seats.

Louisiana crayfish are used in famous Cajun and Creole recipes.

State bird: Brown pelican. "A wonderful bird is the pelican! His bill will hold more than his belican!"—Dixon L. Merritt

Louisiana
Pelican state

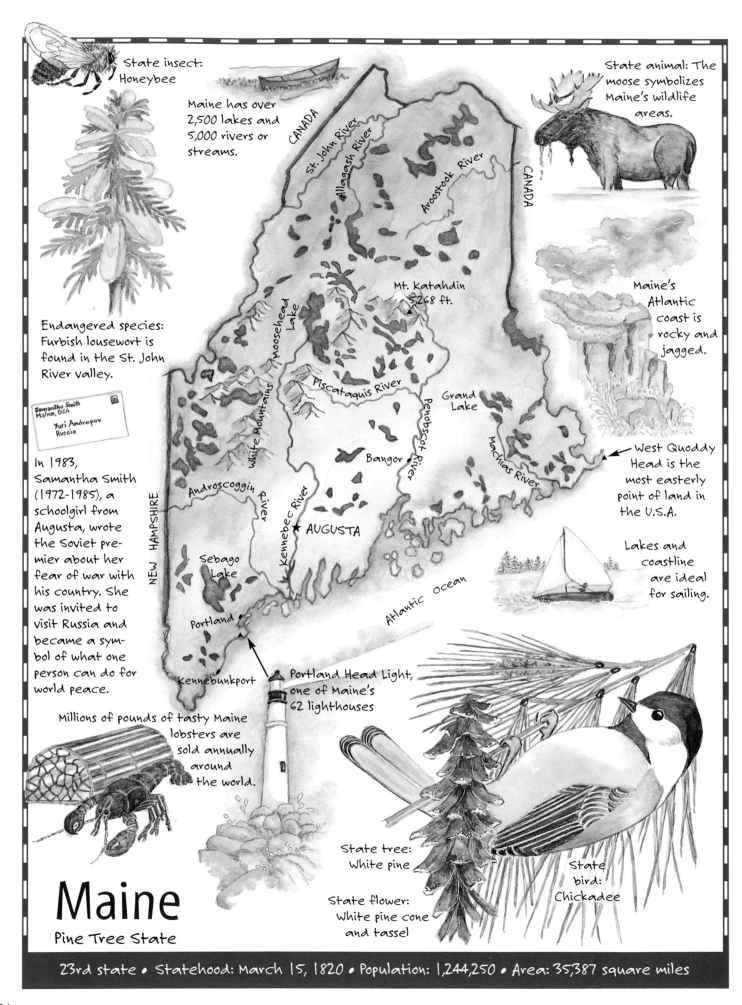

State insect: Honeybee

Maine has over 2,500 lakes and 5,000 rivers or streams.

CANADA

St. John River

Allagash River

Aroostook River

CANADA

State animal: The moose symbolizes Maine's wildlife areas.

Endangered species: Furbish lousewort is found in the St. John River valley.

Mt. Katahdin 5,268 ft.

Moosehead Lake

White Mountains

Piscataquis River

Penobscot River

Grand Lake

Machias River

Maine's Atlantic coast is rocky and jagged.

Samantha Smith
Maine, USA

Yuri Andropov
Russia

In 1983, Samantha Smith (1972-1985), a schoolgirl from Augusta, wrote the Soviet premier about her fear of war with his country. She was invited to visit Russia and became a symbol of what one person can do for world peace.

NEW HAMPSHIRE

Androscoggin River

Kennebec River

Bangor

★ AUGUSTA

West Quoddy Head is the most easterly point of land in the U.S.A.

Lakes and coastline are ideal for sailing.

Sebago Lake

Portland

Atlantic Ocean

Kennebunkport

Portland Head Light, one of Maine's 62 lighthouses

Millions of pounds of tasty Maine lobsters are sold annually around the world.

State tree: White pine

State flower: White pine cone and tassel

State bird: Chickadee

Maine
Pine Tree State

23rd state • Statehood: March 15, 1820 • Population: 1,244,250 • Area: 35,387 square miles

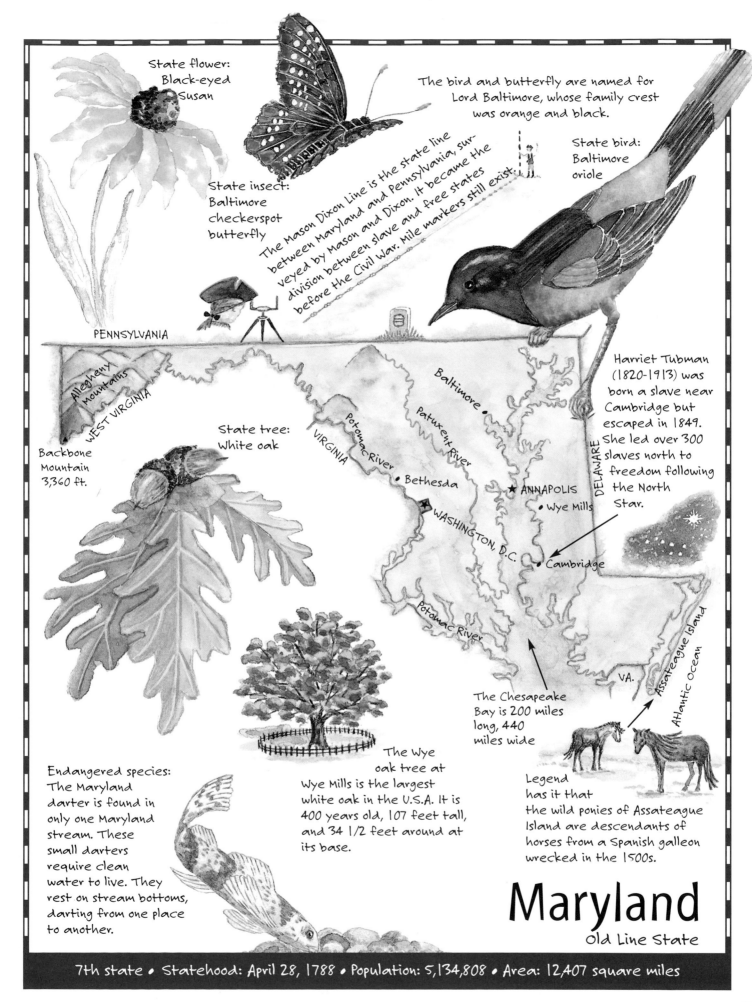

State flower: Black-eyed Susan

State insect: Baltimore checkerspot butterfly

The bird and butterfly are named for Lord Baltimore, whose family crest was orange and black.

State bird: Baltimore oriole

The Mason Dixon Line is the state line between Maryland and Pennsylvania, surveyed by Mason and Dixon. It became the division between slave and free states before the Civil War. Mile markers still exist.

PENNSYLVANIA

Allegheny Mountains

WEST VIRGINIA

Backbone Mountain 3,360 ft.

State tree: White oak

VIRGINIA

Potomac River

Patuxent River

Baltimore •

• Bethesda

WASHINGTON, D.C.

★ ANNAPOLIS

• Wye Mills

DELAWARE

Harriet Tubman (1820-1913) was born a slave near Cambridge but escaped in 1849. She led over 300 slaves north to freedom following the North Star.

• Cambridge

Potomac River

VA.

Assateague Island

Atlantic Ocean

The Chesapeake Bay is 200 miles long, 440 miles wide

The Wye oak tree at Wye Mills is the largest white oak in the U.S.A. It is 400 years old, 107 feet tall, and 34 1/2 feet around at its base.

Legend has it that the wild ponies of Assateague Island are descendants of horses from a Spanish galleon wrecked in the 1500s.

Endangered species: The Maryland darter is found in only one Maryland stream. These small darters require clean water to live. They rest on stream bottoms, darting from one place to another.

Maryland
Old Line State

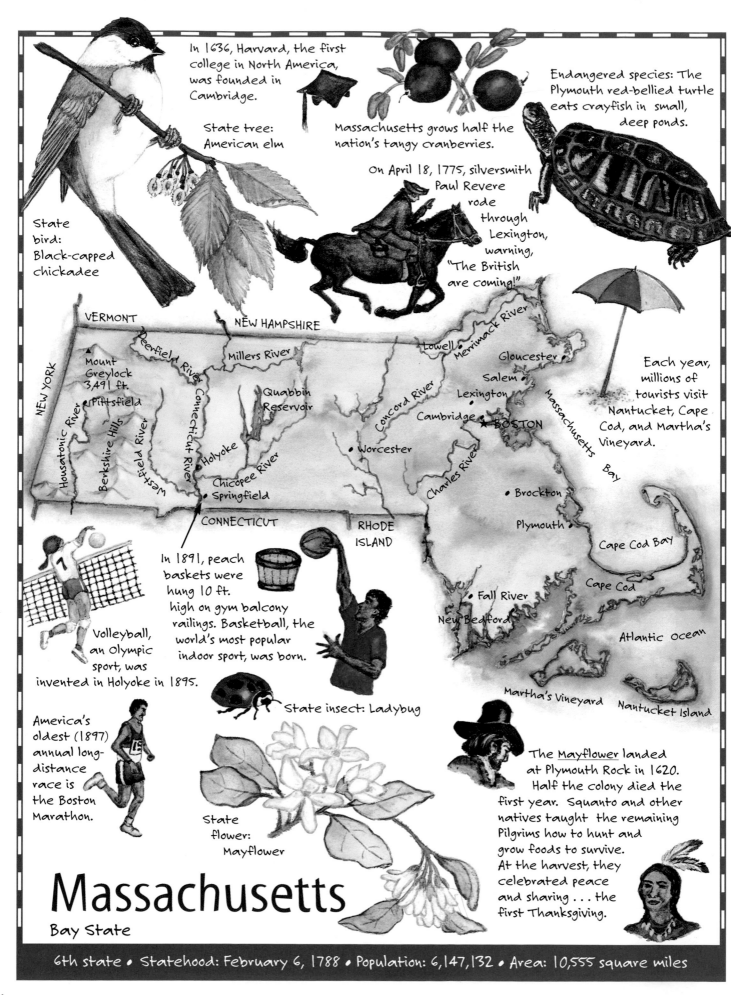

In 1636, Harvard, the first college in North America, was founded in Cambridge.

State tree: American elm

Massachusetts grows half the nation's tangy cranberries.

Endangered species: The Plymouth red-bellied turtle eats crayfish in small, deep ponds.

On April 18, 1775, silversmith Paul Revere rode through Lexington, warning, "The British are coming!"

State bird: Black-capped chickadee

Each year, millions of tourists visit Nantucket, Cape Cod, and Martha's Vineyard.

VERMONT
NEW HAMPSHIRE
NEW YORK
Deerfield River
Millers River
Merrimack River
Lowell
Gloucester
Mount Greylock 3,491 ft.
Pittsfield
Housatonic River
Berkshire Hills
Westfield River
Connecticut River
Quabbin Reservoir
Concord River
Salem
Lexington
Cambridge
★ BOSTON
Massachusetts Bay
Holyoke
Chicopee River
Springfield
Worcester
Charles River
CONNECTICUT
RHODE ISLAND
Brockton
Plymouth
Cape Cod Bay
Cape Cod
Fall River
New Bedford
Atlantic Ocean
Martha's Vineyard
Nantucket Island

In 1891, peach baskets were hung 10 ft. high on gym balcony railings. Basketball, the world's most popular indoor sport, was born.

Volleyball, an Olympic sport, was invented in Holyoke in 1895.

State insect: Ladybug

America's oldest (1897) annual long-distance race is the Boston Marathon.

State flower: Mayflower

The Mayflower landed at Plymouth Rock in 1620. Half the colony died the first year. Squanto and other natives taught the remaining Pilgrims how to hunt and grow foods to survive. At the harvest, they celebrated peace and sharing . . . the first Thanksgiving.

Massachusetts
Bay State

6th state • Statehood: February 6, 1788 • Population: 6,147,132 • Area: 10,555 square miles

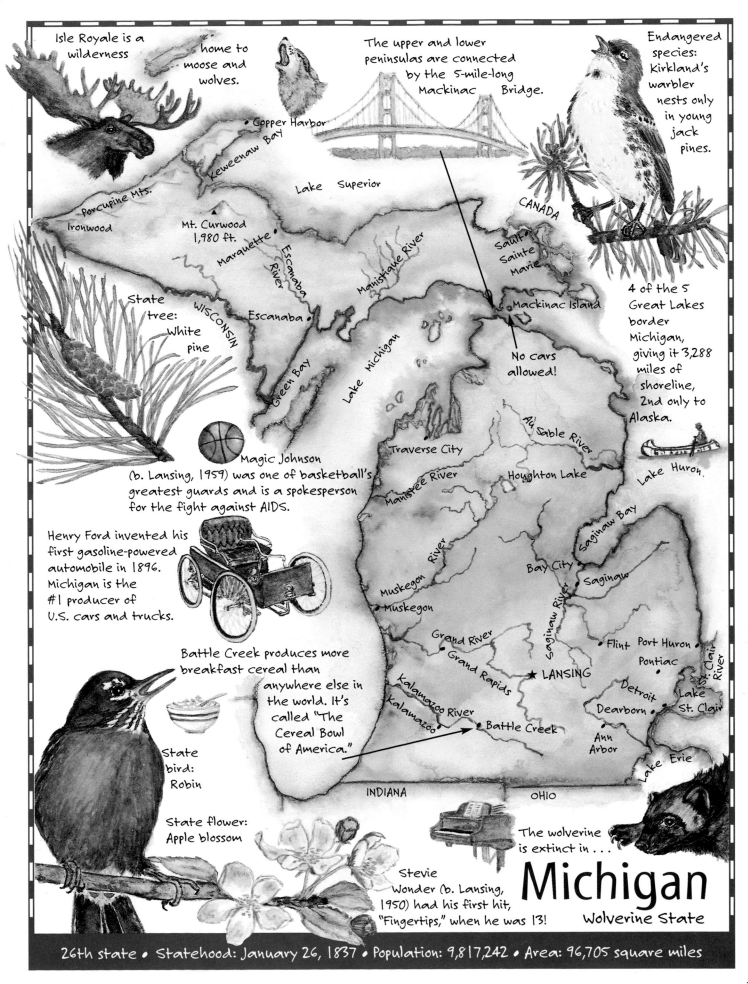

Isle Royale is a wilderness home to moose and wolves.

The upper and lower peninsulas are connected by the 5-mile-long Mackinac Bridge.

Endangered species: Kirkland's warbler nests only in young jack pines.

Copper Harbor

Keweenaw Bay

Lake Superior

CANADA

Porcupine Mts.

Ironwood

Mt. Curwood 1,980 ft.

Marquette

Escanaba River

Manistique River

Sault Sainte Marie

State tree: White pine

WISCONSIN

Escanaba

Mackinac Island

No cars allowed!

4 of the 5 Great Lakes border Michigan, giving it 3,288 miles of shoreline, 2nd only to Alaska.

Green Bay

Lake Michigan

Au Sable River

Lake Huron

Magic Johnson (b. Lansing, 1959) was one of basketball's greatest guards and is a spokesperson for the fight against AIDS.

Traverse City

Manistee River

Houghton Lake

Muskegon River

Saginaw Bay

Henry Ford invented his first gasoline-powered automobile in 1896. Michigan is the #1 producer of U.S. cars and trucks.

Bay City

Saginaw

Saginaw River

Muskegon

Grand River

Flint

Port Huron

Pontiac

St. Clair River

Battle Creek produces more breakfast cereal than anywhere else in the world. It's called "The Cereal Bowl of America."

Grand Rapids

★ LANSING

Detroit

Lake St. Clair

Kalamazoo River

Dearborn

Kalamazoo

Battle Creek

Ann Arbor

State bird: Robin

INDIANA

OHIO

Lake Erie

State flower: Apple blossom

The wolverine is extinct in . . .

Stevie Wonder (b. Lansing, 1950) had his first hit, "Fingertips," when he was 13!

Michigan
Wolverine State

26th state • Statehood: January 26, 1837 • Population: 9,817,242 • Area: 96,705 square miles

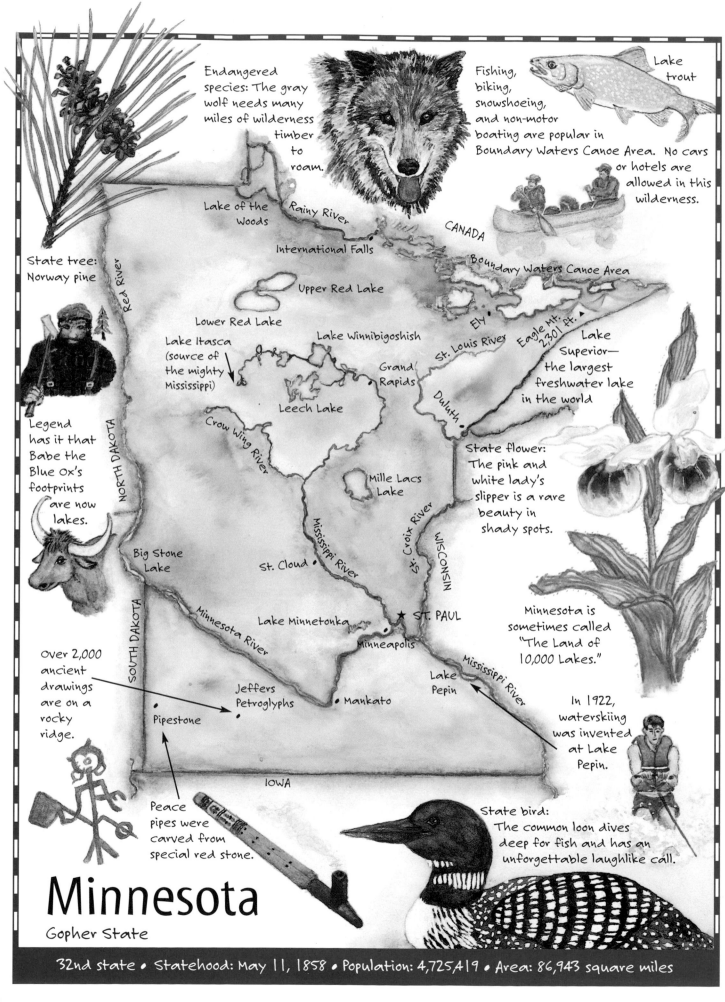

Endangered species: The gray wolf needs many miles of wilderness timber to roam.

Lake trout

Fishing, biking, snowshoeing, and non-motor boating are popular in Boundary Waters Canoe Area. No cars or hotels are allowed in this wilderness.

Lake of the Woods

Rainy River

International Falls

CANADA

Boundary Waters Canoe Area

State tree: Norway pine

Red River

Upper Red Lake

Lower Red Lake

Lake Itasca (source of the mighty Mississippi)

Lake Winnibigoshish

ELY

St. Louis River

Eagle Mt. 2,301 ft.

Lake Superior— the largest freshwater lake in the world

Grand Rapids

Duluth

Leech Lake

Legend has it that Babe the Blue Ox's footprints are now lakes.

NORTH DAKOTA

Crow Wing River

State flower: The pink and white lady's slipper is a rare beauty in shady spots.

Mille Lacs Lake

Big Stone Lake

St. Croix River

WISCONSIN

St. Cloud

Mississippi River

Minnesota is sometimes called "The Land of 10,000 Lakes."

SOUTH DAKOTA

Minnesota River

Lake Minnetonka

★ ST. PAUL

Minneapolis

Lake Pepin

Mississippi River

In 1922, waterskiing was invented at Lake Pepin.

Over 2,000 ancient drawings are on a rocky ridge.

Jeffers Petroglyphs

Pipestone

Mankato

IOWA

Peace pipes were carved from special red stone.

State bird: The common loon dives deep for fish and has an unforgettable laughlike call.

Minnesota

Gopher State

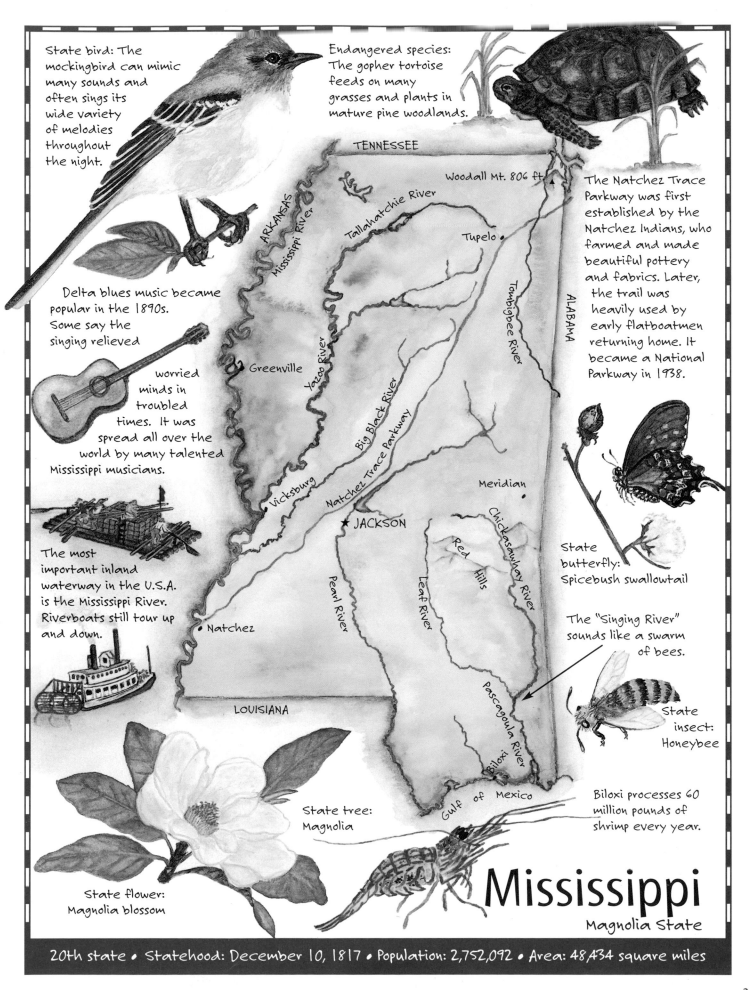

State bird: The mockingbird can mimic many sounds and often sings its wide variety of melodies throughout the night.

Endangered species: The gopher tortoise feeds on many grasses and plants in mature pine woodlands.

Delta blues music became popular in the 1890s. Some say the singing relieved worried minds in troubled times. It was spread all over the world by many talented Mississippi musicians.

The Natchez Trace Parkway was first established by the Natchez Indians, who farmed and made beautiful pottery and fabrics. Later, the trail was heavily used by early flatboatmen returning home. It became a National Parkway in 1938.

The most important inland waterway in the U.S.A. is the Mississippi River. Riverboats still tour up and down.

State butterfly: Spicebush swallowtail

The "Singing River" sounds like a swarm of bees.

State insect: Honeybee

Biloxi processes 60 million pounds of shrimp every year.

TENNESSEE

ARKANSAS

Mississippi River

Tallahatchie River

Woodall Mt. 806 ft.

Tupelo

Tombigbee River

ALABAMA

Yazoo River

Greenville

Big Black River

Natchez Trace Parkway

Vicksburg

Meridian

★ JACKSON

Red Hills

Chickasawhay River

Natchez

Pearl River

Leaf River

Pascagoula River

Biloxi

LOUISIANA

Gulf of Mexico

State tree: Magnolia

State flower: Magnolia blossom

Mississippi
Magnolia State

20th state • Statehood: December 10, 1817 • Population: 2,752,092 • Area: 48,434 square miles

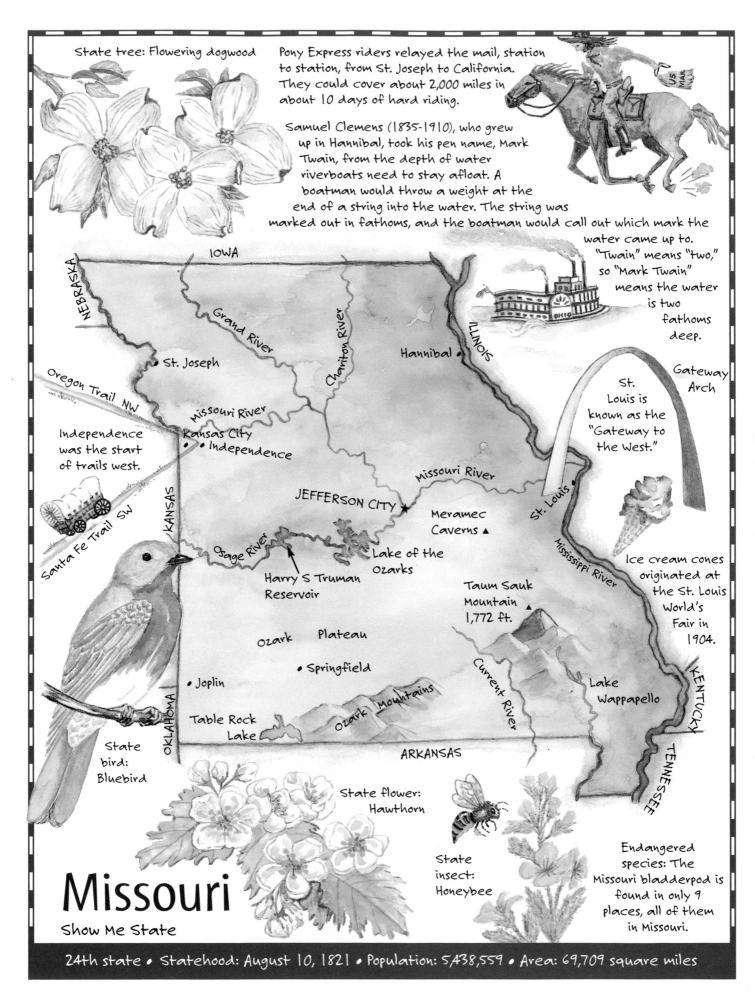

State tree: Flowering dogwood

Pony Express riders relayed the mail, station to station, from St. Joseph to California. They could cover about 2,000 miles in about 10 days of hard riding.

Samuel Clemens (1835-1910), who grew up in Hannibal, took his pen name, Mark Twain, from the depth of water riverboats need to stay afloat. A boatman would throw a weight at the end of a string into the water. The string was marked out in fathoms, and the boatman would call out which mark the water came up to. "Twain" means "two," so "Mark Twain" means the water is two fathoms deep.

IOWA

NEBRASKA

Grand River

Chariton River

St. Joseph

ILLINOIS

Hannibal

OHIO

Oregon Trail NW

Independence was the start of trails west.

Missouri River

Kansas City

Independence

KANSAS

Santa Fe Trail SW

Gateway Arch

St. Louis is known as the "Gateway to the West."

JEFFERSON CITY

Meramec Caverns ▲

Missouri River

St. Louis

Osage River

Harry S Truman Reservoir

Lake of the Ozarks

Mississippi River

Ice cream cones originated at the St. Louis World's Fair in 1904.

Taum Sauk Mountain 1,772 ft. ▲

Ozark   Plateau

Current River

Springfield

Lake Wappapello

Joplin

KENTUCKY

OKLAHOMA

Ozark Mountains

Table Rock Lake

ARKANSAS

TENNESSEE

State bird: Bluebird

State flower: Hawthorn

State insect: Honeybee

Endangered species: The Missouri bladderpod is found in only 9 places, all of them in Missouri.

Missouri

Show Me State

24th state • Statehood: August 10, 1821 • Population: 5,438,559 • Area: 69,709 square miles

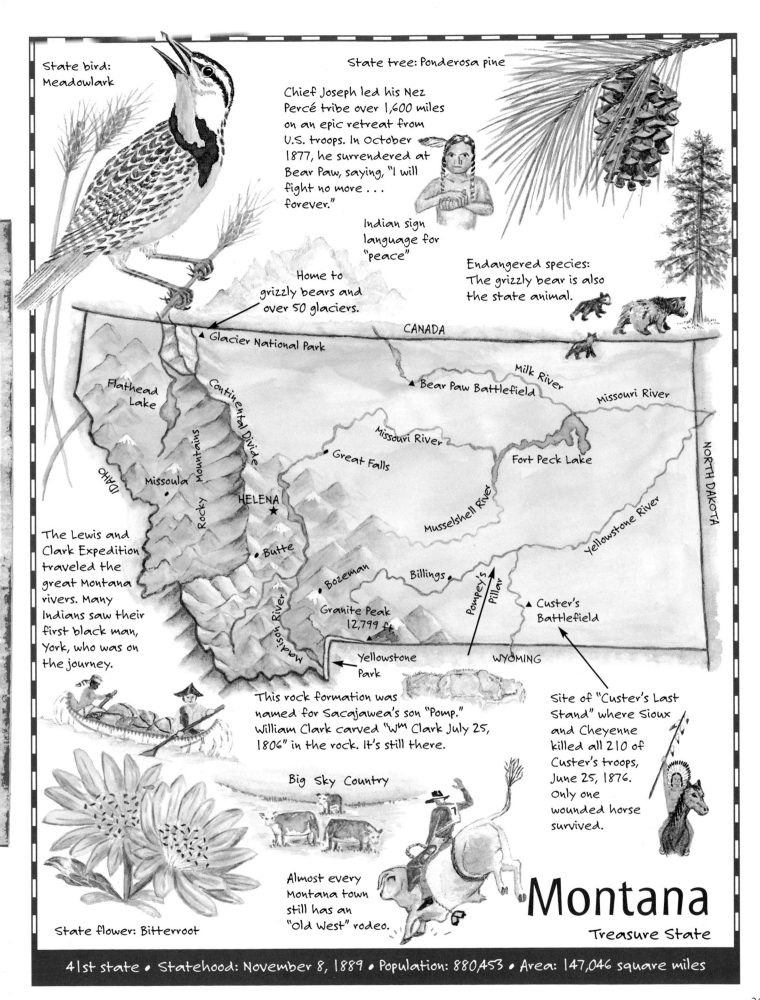

State bird: Meadowlark

State tree: Ponderosa pine

Chief Joseph led his Nez Percé tribe over 1,600 miles on an epic retreat from U.S. troops. In October 1877, he surrendered at Bear Paw, saying, "I will fight no more . . . forever."

Indian sign language for "peace"

Endangered species: The grizzly bear is also the state animal.

Home to grizzly bears and over 50 glaciers.

CANADA

Glacier National Park

Bear Paw Battlefield

Milk River

Missouri River

Flathead Lake

Continental Divide

Missouri River

Great Falls

Fort Peck Lake

NORTH DAKOTA

IDAHO

Rocky Mountains

Missoula

HELENA

Musselshell River

Yellowstone River

Butte

The Lewis and Clark Expedition traveled the great Montana rivers. Many Indians saw their first black man, York, who was on the journey.

Madison River

Bozeman

Billings

Pompey's Pillar

Custer's Battlefield

Granite Peak 12,799 ft

WYOMING

Yellowstone Park

This rock formation was named for Sacajawea's son "Pomp." William Clark carved "Wm Clark July 25, 1806" in the rock. It's still there.

Site of "Custer's Last Stand" where Sioux and Cheyenne killed all 210 of Custer's troops, June 25, 1876. Only one wounded horse survived.

Big Sky Country

State flower: Bitterroot

Almost every Montana town still has an "Old West" rodeo.

Montana
Treasure State

41st state • Statehood: November 8, 1889 • Population: 880,453 • Area: 147,046 square miles

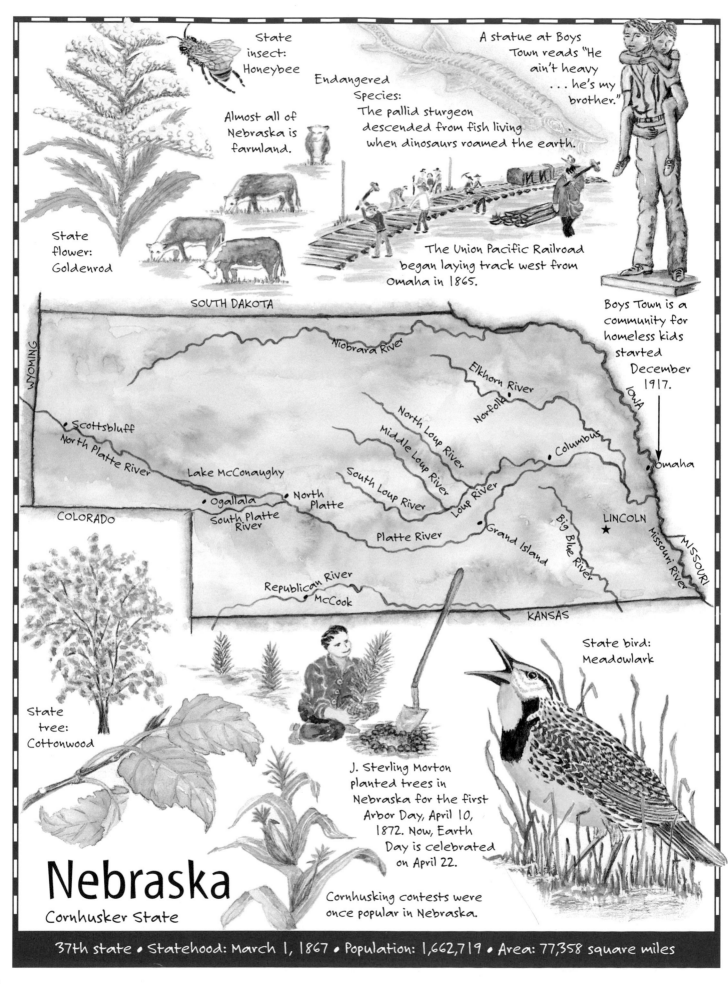

State insect: Honeybee

Almost all of Nebraska is farmland.

Endangered Species: The pallid sturgeon descended from fish living when dinosaurs roamed the earth.

A statue at Boys Town reads "He ain't heavy . . . he's my brother."

State flower: Goldenrod

The Union Pacific Railroad began laying track west from Omaha in 1865.

Boys Town is a community for homeless kids started December 1917.

SOUTH DAKOTA

WYOMING

Niobrara River

Elkhorn River

Norfolk

IOWA

North Loup River

Scottsbluff

Middle Loup River

Columbus

North Platte River

Lake McConaughy

South Loup River

Loup River

Omaha

Ogallala

North Platte

Platte River

Big Blue River

LINCOLN

MISSOURI

COLORADO

South Platte River

Grand Island

Missouri River

Republican River

McCook

KANSAS

State tree: Cottonwood

State bird: Meadowlark

J. Sterling Morton planted trees in Nebraska for the first Arbor Day, April 10, 1872. Now, Earth Day is celebrated on April 22.

Nebraska
Cornhusker State

Cornhusking contests were once popular in Nebraska.

37th state • Statehood: March 1, 1867 • Population: 1,662,719 • Area: 77,358 square miles

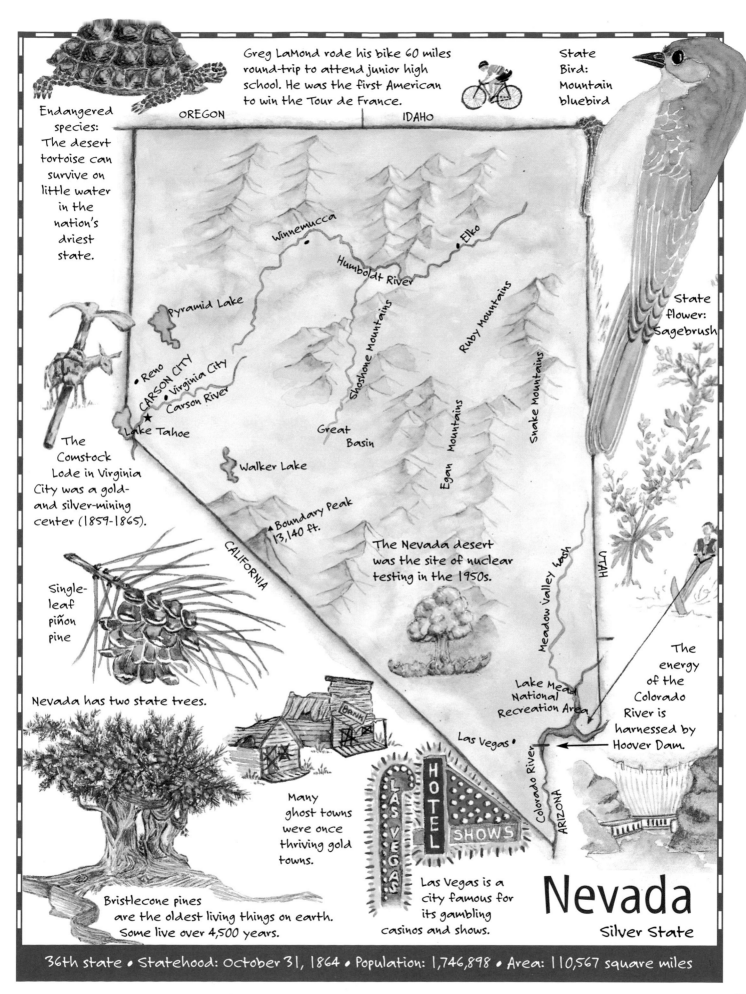

Endangered species: The desert tortoise can survive on little water in the nation's driest state.

Greg LaMond rode his bike 60 miles round-trip to attend junior high school. He was the first American to win the Tour de France.

State Bird: Mountain bluebird

OREGON

IDAHO

State flower: Sagebrush

The Comstock Lode in Virginia City was a gold- and silver-mining center (1859-1865).

Winnemucca

Pyramid Lake

Humboldt River

Elko

Shoshone Mountains

Ruby Mountains

Reno
CARSON CITY
Virginia City
Carson River
Lake Tahoe

Egan Mountains

Snake Mountains

Great Basin

Walker Lake

Boundary Peak 13,140 ft.

CALIFORNIA

UTAH

The Nevada desert was the site of nuclear testing in the 1950s.

Single-leaf piñon pine

Meadow Valley Wash

The energy of the Colorado River is harnessed by Hoover Dam.

Nevada has two state trees.

Lake Mead National Recreation Area

Las Vegas

BANK

Colorado River

ARIZONA

Many ghost towns were once thriving gold towns.

LAS VEGAS HOTEL SHOWS

Nevada
Silver State

Las Vegas is a city famous for its gambling casinos and shows.

Bristlecone pines are the oldest living things on earth. Some live over 4,500 years.

36th state • Statehood: October 31, 1864 • Population: 1,746,898 • Area: 110,567 square miles

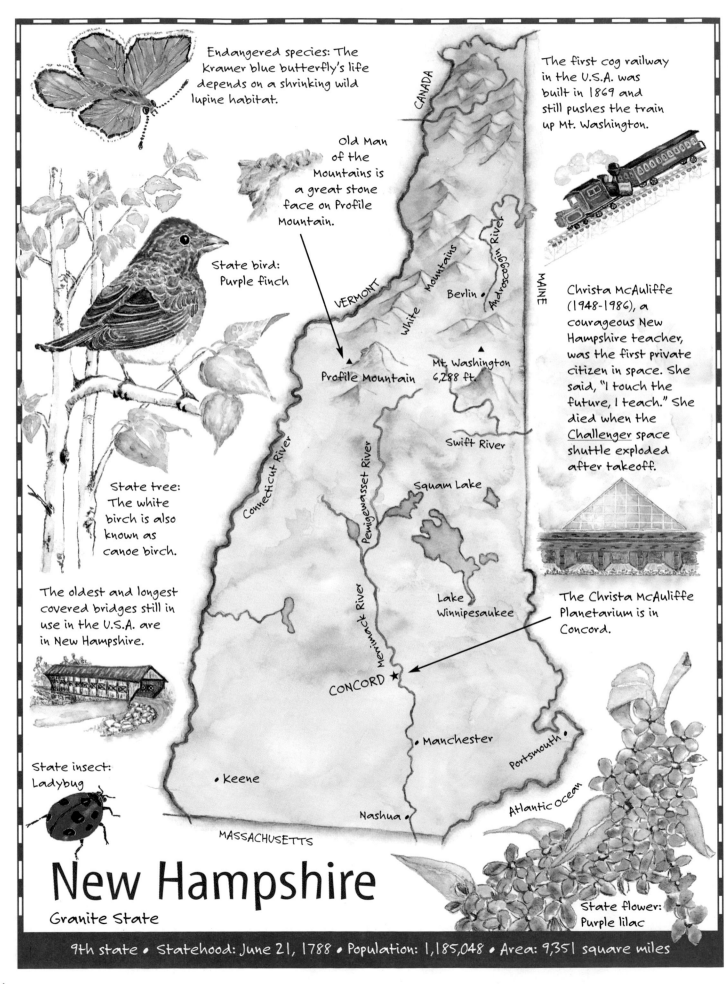

Endangered species: The Kramer blue butterfly's life depends on a shrinking wild lupine habitat.

Old Man of the Mountains is a great stone face on Profile Mountain.

The first cog railway in the U.S.A. was built in 1869 and still pushes the train up Mt. Washington.

CANADA

VERMONT

MAINE

White Mountains

Berlin

Androscoggin River

State bird: Purple finch

Profile Mountain

Mt. Washington 6,288 ft.

Christa McAuliffe (1948-1986), a courageous New Hampshire teacher, was the first private citizen in space. She said, "I touch the future, I teach." She died when the Challenger space shuttle exploded after takeoff.

Swift River

Connecticut River

Pemigewasset River

Squam Lake

State tree: The white birch is also known as canoe birch.

Lake Winnipesaukee

The Christa McAuliffe Planetarium is in Concord.

The oldest and longest covered bridges still in use in the U.S.A. are in New Hampshire.

Merrimack River

CONCORD ★

State insect: Ladybug

• Manchester

Portsmouth •

• Keene

Atlantic Ocean

Nashua •

MASSACHUSETTS

New Hampshire

Granite State

State flower: Purple lilac

9th state • Statehood: June 21, 1788 • Population: 1,185,048 • Area: 9,351 square miles

34

State bird: Goldfinch

State tree: Red oak bark is rich in tannin, used for tanning leather.

The Garden State is famous for its Jersey tomatoes.

New Jersey is a leader in producing chemicals.

State dinosaur: Hadrosaur, the first dinosaur skeleton discovered in North America, was found near Haddonfield in 1858.

State insect: Honeybees are vital for pollinating gardens.

PENNSYLVANIA

NEW YORK

Appalachian Mountains

Lake Hopatcong

Musconetcong River

Passaic River

Hackensack River

Hudson River

Newark • Hoboken Jersey City

Piedmont Plateau

• Princeton

★ TRENTON

Delaware River

Tom's River

• Camden
  Haddonfield

Mullica River

Great Egg Harbor River

Jersey Shore Resorts

Atlantic Ocean

DELAWARE

The Pine Barrens is a wilderness of bogs, salt marshes, and swamps.

Delaware Bay

• Cape May

The Sandy Hook Lighthouse has been guiding ships into port since 1763.

Many people vacation on the white sandy beaches of the Jersey shore.

Endangered species: Roseate tern

It needs isolated beaches for concealed nests.

Atlantic City is famous for its wooden boardwalk and saltwater taffy.

State flower: Violet

New Jersey
Garden State

State tree: Piñon pine

Gallup hosts the Intertribal Indian Ceremonial every August.

Hot air balloons from all over the world come to Albuquerque in mid-October.

Endangered species: New Mexican ridgenose rattlesnakes hide out in remote pine-oak woodlands.

Shiprock, or Tsé Bit'a'i, is a rock formation sacred to the Navajo.

State insect: Tarantula hawk wasps lay eggs inside spiders.

New Mexico grows the most chilies in the U.S.A.

In 1950, a bear cub was rescued from a forest fire; he became Smoky the Bear.

UTAH
Four Corners
COLORADO
OKLAHOMA
Farmington
San Juan River
Wheeler Peak 13,161 ft.
Chaco Culture National Historic Park
Coyote
Taos
Canadian River
Los Alamos
★ SANTA FE
Gallup
Continental Divide
Albuquerque
Santa Fe was founded in 1610 and is the oldest state capital.
Clovis
Rocky Mountains
Lincoln National Forest
Pecos River
Mogollon
Roswell
Gila River
Rio Grande
Silver City
White Sands National Monument
Las Cruces
Carlsbad Caverns
Columbus
TEXAS
ARIZONA
MEXICO

The sand dunes are so white they glisten like snow fields.

At dusk, tens of thousands of bats emerge from limestone caverns in 24 miles of passages to feast on millions of bugs. There are many caves. The Big Room is the largest natural cave in the world.

State flower: Yucca

State bird: The roadrunner prefers to run (15 m.p.h.) rather than fly.

New Mexico
Land of Enchantment

47th state • Statehood: January 6, 1912 • Population: 1,736,931 • Area: 121,598 square miles

Lake Placid was the site of the 1932 and the 1980 Winter Olympics.

State Flower: Rose

Endangered species: The American hart's-tongue fern grows in the cool, moist soil of limestone sinkholes.

Mary Jemison was a white child captured by a Seneca tribe in 1755. She refused later offers to return to a white settlement.

The Statue of Liberty was a gift from France in 1884. It stands in New York Harbor.

State insect: Ladybug

Canada and the U.S.A. share the world's most famous waterfall.

CANADA

Lake Champlain

Thousand Islands

Lake Placid

Mt. Marcy 5,344 ft.

Adirondack Mountains

Lake George

Lake Ontario

Niagara Falls

CANADA

Buffalo

East Aurora

Lake Erie

Rochester

Syracuse

Oneida Lake

Utica

Mohawk River

VERMONT

Genesee River

Finger Lakes

Cooperstown

Susquehanna River

Catskill Mountains

ALBANY

MASSACHUSETTS

Elmira

Binghamton

PENNSYLVANIA

Hudson River

Poughkeepsie

CONNECTICUT

Cooperstown is home of The National Baseball Hall of Fame.

West Point

Coney Island is a beach resort known for its boardwalk and hot dogs.

NEW JERSEY

New York City

Long Island Sound

Long Island

State bird: Bluebird

Staten Island

Atlantic Ocean

Opened in 1932, in downtown New York City, this theater seats 5,883.

RADIO CITY

From 1892 to 1954, over 12 million immigrants passed through Ellis Island Center.

State tree: The sugar maple is the source of maple syrup and candy, as well as blazing autumn colors.

The United Nations headquarters are in New York City.

New York
Empire State

11th state • Statehood: July 26, 1788 • Population: 18,175,301 • Area: 54,471 square miles

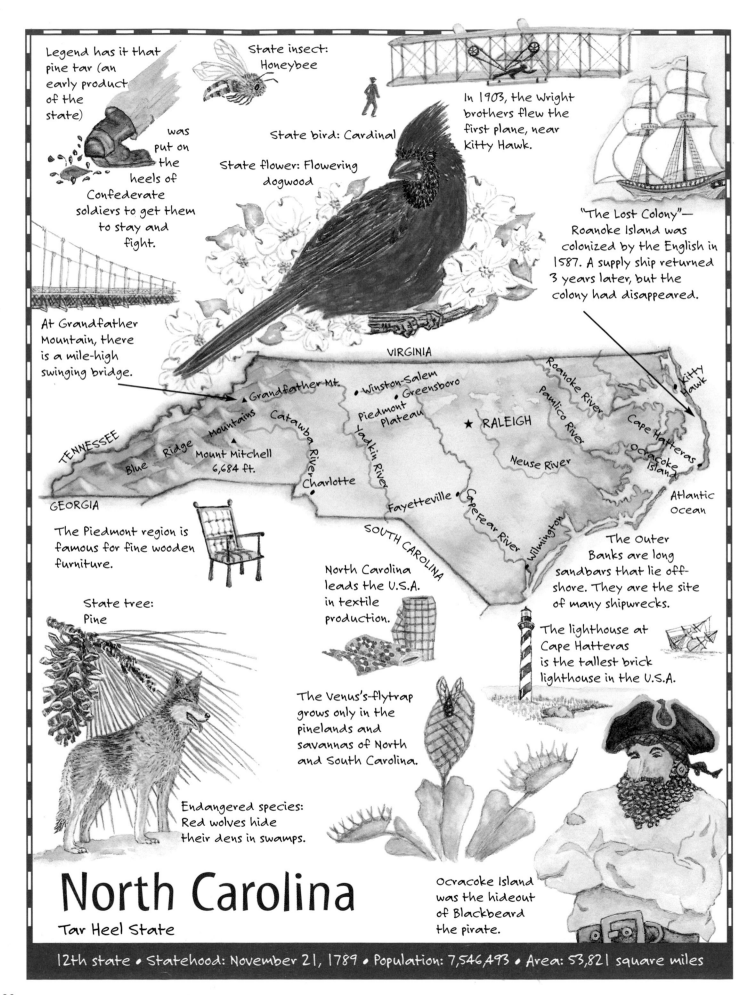

Legend has it that pine tar (an early product of the state) was put on the heels of Confederate soldiers to get them to stay and fight.

State insect: Honeybee

In 1903, the Wright brothers flew the first plane, near Kitty Hawk.

State bird: Cardinal

State flower: Flowering dogwood

"The Lost Colony"— Roanoke Island was colonized by the English in 1587. A supply ship returned 3 years later, but the colony had disappeared.

At Grandfather Mountain, there is a mile-high swinging bridge.

VIRGINIA

Winston-Salem
Greensboro
Roanoke River
Kitty Hawk
Piedmont Plateau
★ RALEIGH
Pamlico River
Cape Hatteras
Grandfather Mt.
Catawba River
Yadkin River
Neuse River
Ocracoke Island
TENNESSEE
Blue Ridge Mountains
Mount Mitchell 6,684 ft.
Atlantic Ocean
GEORGIA
Charlotte
Fayetteville
Cape Fear River
Wilmington
SOUTH CAROLINA

The Piedmont region is famous for fine wooden furniture.

North Carolina leads the U.S.A. in textile production.

The Outer Banks are long sandbars that lie off-shore. They are the site of many shipwrecks.

The lighthouse at Cape Hatteras is the tallest brick lighthouse in the U.S.A.

State tree: Pine

The Venus's-flytrap grows only in the pinelands and savannas of North and South Carolina.

Endangered species: Red wolves hide their dens in swamps.

North Carolina
Tar Heel State

Ocracoke Island was the hideout of Blackbeard the pirate.

12th state • Statehood: November 21, 1789 • Population: 7,546,493 • Area: 53,821 square miles

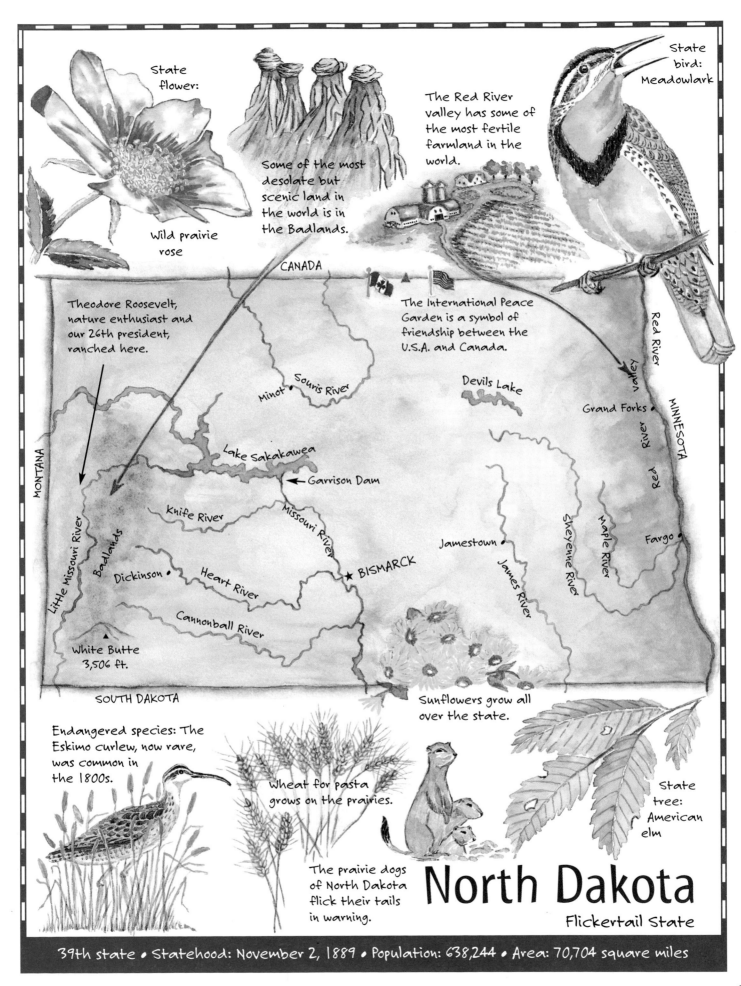

State flower:

Wild prairie rose

Some of the most desolate but scenic land in the world is in the Badlands.

The Red River valley has some of the most fertile farmland in the world.

State bird: Meadowlark

CANADA

Theodore Roosevelt, nature enthusiast and our 26th president, ranched here.

The International Peace Garden is a symbol of friendship between the U.S.A. and Canada.

MONTANA

Minot • Souris River

Devils Lake

Red River Valley

Grand Forks •

MINNESOTA

Lake Sakakawea

← Garrison Dam

Knife River

Missouri River

Jamestown •

Sheyenne River

Maple River

Red River

Fargo •

Badlands

Little Missouri River

Dickinson •

Heart River

→ BISMARCK

James River

Cannonball River

White Butte 3,506 ft.

SOUTH DAKOTA

Sunflowers grow all over the state.

Endangered species: The Eskimo curlew, now rare, was common in the 1800s.

Wheat for pasta grows on the prairies.

The prairie dogs of North Dakota flick their tails in warning.

State tree: American elm

North Dakota
Flickertail State

Endangered species: The lakeside daisy grows in limestone quarries.

John Chapman (Johnny Appleseed) planted hundreds of acres of apple orchards in Ohio.

Raw materials imported on Ohio's rail, water, and truck routes are manufactured into products and exported on the same routes.

The Pro Football Hall of Fame is in Canton.

About 2,000 years ago, Indian Mound Builders came to the Ohio Valley and shaped over 10,000 burial mounds. The Serpentine Mound near Hillsboro is more than 1/4 mile long.

Seven U.S. presidents were born in Ohio: Grant Hayes Garfield Harrison McKinley Taft Harding

The Ohio River is navigable all year long. It empties into the Mississippi.

MICHIGAN

Toledo

Maumee River

Sandusky River

Sandusky

Lake Erie

Cleveland

Akron

Cuyahoga River

Youngstown

Canton

PENNSYLVANIA

Campbell Hill 1,550 ft.

INDIANA

Great Miami River

Dayton

Little Miami River

Cincinnati

Hillsboro

Scioto River

COLUMBUS

Muskingum River

Marietta

Ohio River

WEST VIRGINIA

KENTUCKY

Ohio River

SEAL OF THE PRESIDENT OF THE UNITED STATES

State flower: Scarlet carnation

An Ohio architect, Maya Ying Lin, designed the Vietnam Memorial in Washington, D.C.

State bird: Cardinal

State insect: Ladybug

State tree: Buckeye

Ohio
Buckeye State

17th state • Statehood: March 1, 1803 • Population: 11,209,493 • Area: 44,828 square miles

40

Oil is found in every Oklahoma county. There is even an oil pump on the front lawn of the state capitol.

Endangered species: Piping plovers nest on sandy river beaches.

National Cowboy Hall of Fame is in Oklahoma City.

"The Trail of Tears"— Between 1830 and 1842, Native Americans were made to travel over 1,000 miles from the southeast to resettle in Oklahoma.

Will Rogers (1879-1935) entertained with rope tricks and witty remarks. He said, "I never met a man I didn't like."

COLORADO
KANSAS
NEW MEXICO
TEXAS
MISSOURI
ARKANSAS
TEXAS

Black Mesa 4,973 ft.
North Canadian River
Cimarron River
• Enid
Arkansas River
Oolagah Lake
Tulsa •
Chisholm Trail
• Guthrie
Muskogee •
★ OKLAHOMA CITY
Washita River
Canadian River
Wichita Mountains
Ouachita Mountains
Red River
Lake Texoma

State bird: Scissor-tailed flycatcher

The Red River's color comes from the clay and minerals in the water.

State tree: Redbud

In the 1870s, the Chisholm Trail was a major route to drive cattle north to the Kansas railroads.

State flower: Mistletoe (a tree parasite)

At noon on April 22, a pistol shot started the 1889 land run. 50,000 settlers moved into Oklahoma overnight. Some folks snuck in "sooner," before the land was opened.

State wildflower: Blanketflower

Oklahoma
Sooner State

46th state • Statehood: November 16, 1907 • Population: 3,346,713 • Area: 69,903 square miles

Endangered species:
The northern
spotted owl lives in
old-growth forests.

State insect:
Oregon
swallowtail

Beaver were once abundant
in Oregon waterways.
In the 1800s,
thousands
of pelts were
used each year to make
men's hats.

State tree:
Douglas fir

Ft. Clatsop

Sea
lion
caves

WASHINGTON

Columbia River

Portland

SALEM

Mt. Hood
11,239 ft.

Willamette River

Willamette Valley

John

Day

River

Blue Mountains

Hell's
Canyon,
on the
Snake
River, is
the
deepest
in the U.S.A.
(8,023 ft.).

Snake River

IDAHO

The
Oregon
Trail was

Pacific
Ocean

Coast
Range

Eugene

Cascade
Mountains

In 1902, the
largest meteorite
in the U.S.A. was
found in the
Willamette
Valley.

Malheur Lake

Harney Lake

a 2,000-
mile wagon
trail from
Missouri to
the Pacific
Ocean. Its
ruts can
still be
seen in
some
places.

Crater Lake

Klamath   Mountains

Upper Klamath Lake

CALIFORNIA

NEVADA

Oregon harvests more
timber than
any other
state.

Crater Lake is the deepest
in the U.S.A. (1,932 ft.).

State bird:
Meadowlark

Oregon
Beaver State

State
flower:
Oregon grape

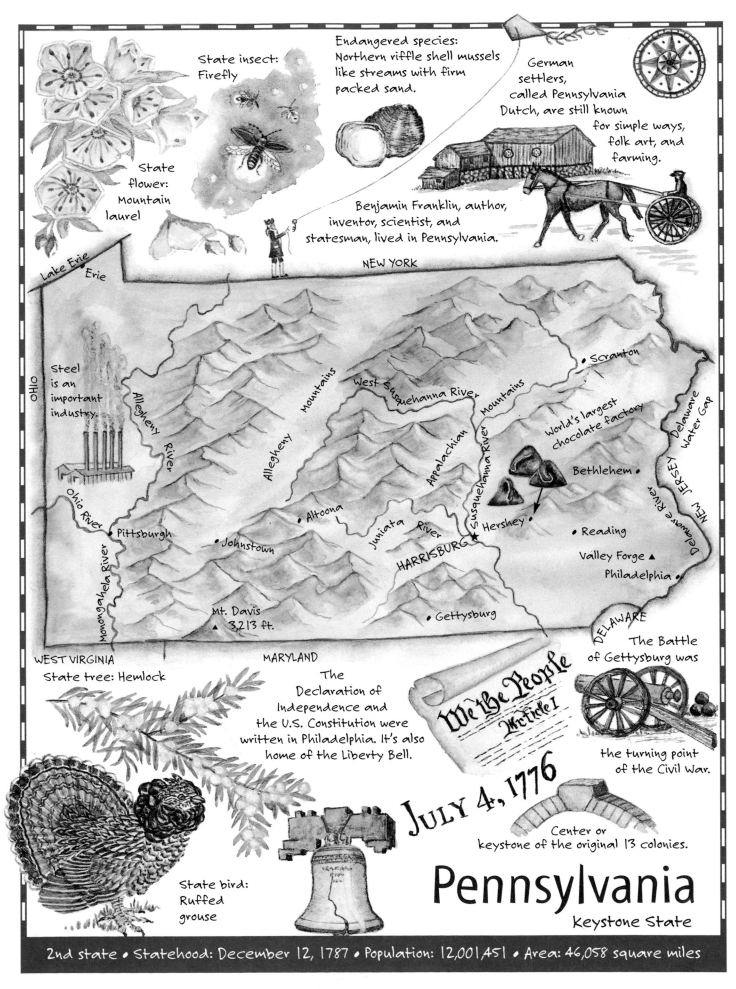

State insect: Firefly

Endangered species: Northern riffle shell mussels like streams with firm packed sand.

German settlers, called Pennsylvania Dutch, are still known for simple ways, folk art, and farming.

State flower: Mountain laurel

Benjamin Franklin, author, inventor, scientist, and statesman, lived in Pennsylvania.

NEW YORK

Lake Erie

Erie

OHIO

Steel is an important industry.

Allegheny River

Allegheny Mountains

West Susquehanna River

Scranton

Appalachian Mountains

Delaware Water Gap

World's largest chocolate factory

Bethlehem

NEW JERSEY

Delaware River

Susquehanna River

Altoona

Ohio River

Pittsburgh

Johnstown

Juniata River

Hershey

Reading

Valley Forge ▲

Philadelphia

Monongahela River

HARRISBURG

Mt. Davis ▲ 3,213 ft.

Gettysburg

DELAWARE

The Battle of Gettysburg was the turning point of the Civil War.

WEST VIRGINIA

MARYLAND

State tree: Hemlock

The Declaration of Independence and the U.S. Constitution were written in Philadelphia. It's also home of the Liberty Bell.

We the People Article I

JULY 4, 1776

Center or keystone of the original 13 colonies.

State bird: Ruffed grouse

Pennsylvania

Keystone State

2nd state • Statehood: December 12, 1787 • Population: 12,001,451 • Area: 46,058 square miles

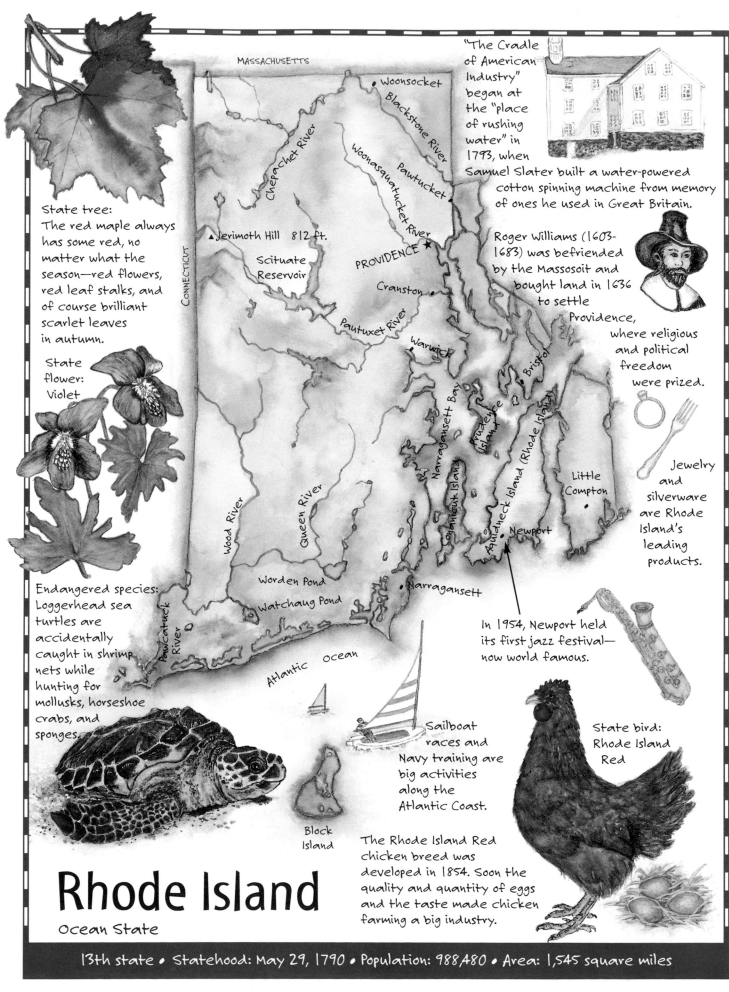

MASSACHUSETTS

• Woonsocket

Blackstone River

Chepachet River

Woonasquatucket River

Pawtucket

▲ Jerimoth Hill 812 ft.

Scituate Reservoir

PROVIDENCE ★

CONNECTICUT

Cranston •

Pautuxet River

Warwick

Narragansett Bay

Prudence Island

Bristol

Conanicut Island

Aquidneck Island (Rhode Island)

Little Compton •

Wood River

Queen River

Newport •

Worden Pond

Watchaug Pond

• Narragansett

Pawcatuck River

Atlantic   Ocean

Block Island

"The Cradle of American Industry" began at the "place of rushing water" in 1793, when Samuel Slater built a water-powered cotton spinning machine from memory of ones he used in Great Britain.

Roger Williams (1603-1683) was befriended by the Massosoit and bought land in 1636 to settle Providence, where religious and political freedom were prized.

Jewelry and silverware are Rhode Island's leading products.

State tree: The red maple always has some red, no matter what the season—red flowers, red leaf stalks, and of course brilliant scarlet leaves in autumn.

State flower: Violet

Endangered species: Loggerhead sea turtles are accidentally caught in shrimp nets while hunting for mollusks, horseshoe crabs, and sponges.

In 1954, Newport held its first jazz festival—now world famous.

Sailboat races and Navy training are big activities along the Atlantic Coast.

State bird: Rhode Island Red

The Rhode Island Red chicken breed was developed in 1854. Soon the quality and quantity of eggs and the taste made chicken farming a big industry.

Rhode Island

Ocean State

13th state • Statehood: May 29, 1790 • Population: 988,480 • Area: 1,545 square miles

44

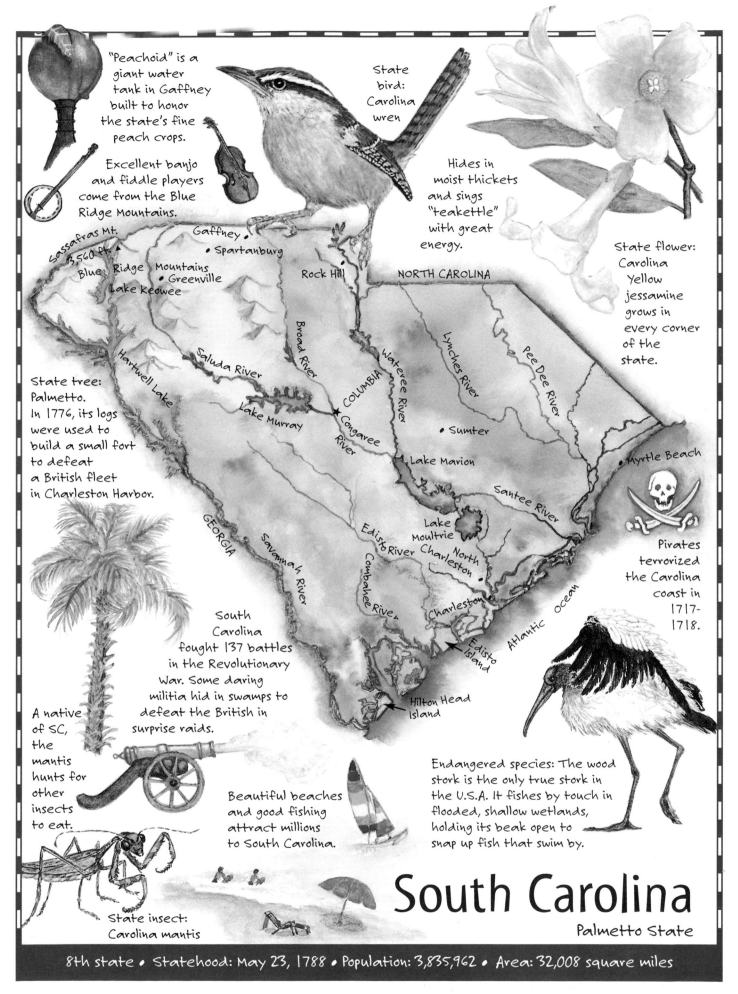

"Peachoid" is a giant water tank in Gaffney built to honor the state's fine peach crops.

Excellent banjo and fiddle players come from the Blue Ridge Mountains.

State bird: Carolina wren

Hides in moist thickets and sings "teakettle" with great energy.

State flower: Carolina Yellow jessamine grows in every corner of the state.

State tree: Palmetto. In 1776, its logs were used to build a small fort to defeat a British fleet in Charleston Harbor.

Pirates terrorized the Carolina coast in 1717-1718.

A native of SC, the mantis hunts for other insects to eat.

South Carolina fought 137 battles in the Revolutionary War. Some daring militia hid in swamps to defeat the British in surprise raids.

Beautiful beaches and good fishing attract millions to South Carolina.

Endangered species: The wood stork is the only true stork in the U.S.A. It fishes by touch in flooded, shallow wetlands, holding its beak open to snap up fish that swim by.

State insect: Carolina mantis

South Carolina
Palmetto State

Map labels: Sassafras Mt. 3,560 ft., Gaffney, Spartanburg, Greenville, Rock Hill, NORTH CAROLINA, Blue Ridge Mountains, Lake Keowee, Hartwell Lake, Saluda River, Broad River, Wateree River, Lynches River, Pee Dee River, COLUMBIA, Congaree River, Lake Murray, Sumter, Lake Marion, Santee River, GEORGIA, Savannah River, Edisto River, Combahee River, Lake Moultrie, North Charleston, Charleston, Myrtle Beach, Edisto Island, Atlantic Ocean, Hilton Head Island

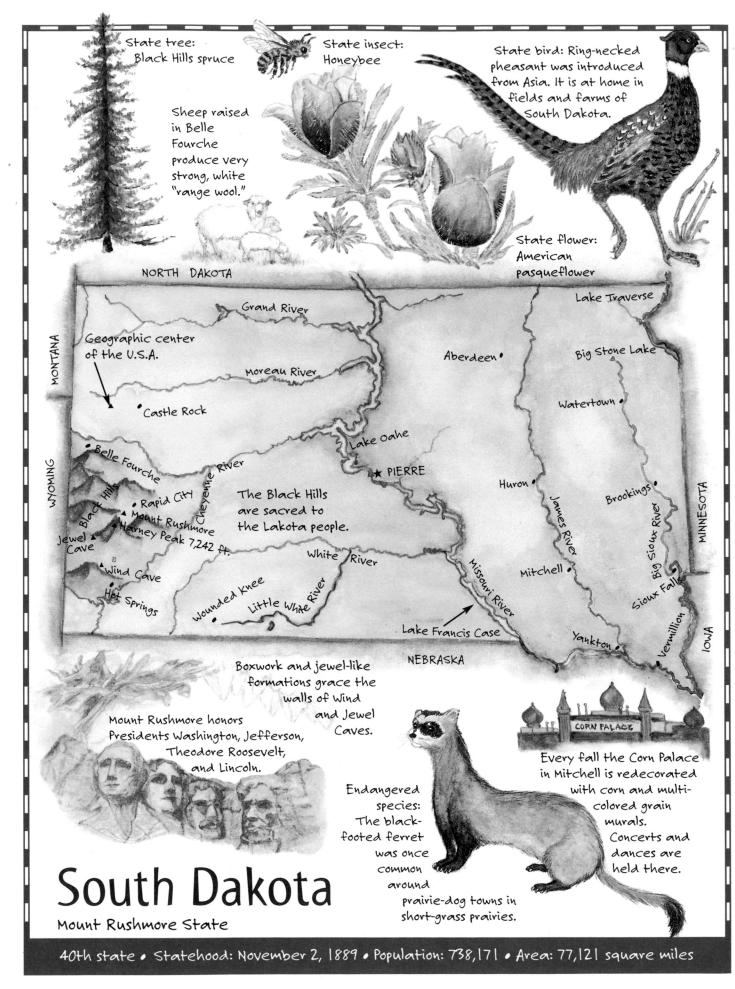

State tree: Black Hills spruce

State insect: Honeybee

State bird: Ring-necked pheasant was introduced from Asia. It is at home in fields and farms of South Dakota.

Sheep raised in Belle Fourche produce very strong, white "range wool."

State flower: American pasqueflower

NORTH DAKOTA

MONTANA

Grand River

Geographic center of the U.S.A.

Moreau River

Lake Traverse

Aberdeen •

Big Stone Lake

Watertown •

• Castle Rock

Lake Oahe

★ PIERRE

Huron •

Brookings •

WYOMING

• Belle Fourche

Cheyenne River

The Black Hills are sacred to the Lakota people.

James River

Big Sioux River

MINNESOTA

Black Hills

• Rapid City

▲ Mount Rushmore

▲ Harney Peak 7,242 ft.

Mitchell •

Jewel Cave ▲

White River

Sioux Falls

Wind Cave ▲

Missouri River

Hot Springs

Wounded Knee

Little White River

Lake Francis Case

Yankton •

Vermillion

IOWA

NEBRASKA

Boxwork and jewel-like formations grace the walls of Wind and Jewel Caves.

Mount Rushmore honors Presidents Washington, Jefferson, Theodore Roosevelt, and Lincoln.

CORN PALACE

Endangered species: The black-footed ferret was once common around prairie-dog towns in short-grass prairies.

Every fall the Corn Palace in Mitchell is redecorated with corn and multi-colored grain murals. Concerts and dances are held there.

South Dakota

Mount Rushmore State

40th state • Statehood: November 2, 1889 • Population: 738,171 • Area: 77,121 square miles

46

State tree: Tulip poplar

State bird: The mockingbird is a talented and varied singer in a state famous for different kinds of music: bluegrass, rock 'n' roll, blues, and country.

Davy Crockett was a frontiersman and a gifted storyteller. His motto was "Be always sure you're right—then go ahead."

(1786-1836)

In December 1811, a violent earthquake made the Mississippi River change course, and a giant wave created Reelfoot Lake.

State insects: Firefly and ladybug

KENTUCKY

VIRGINIA

MISSOURI

Reelfoot Lake

Cumberland River

Cumberland Mts.

Appalachian Mts.

ARKANSAS

Mississippi River

Tennessee River

Cumberland Plateau

Oak Ridge

Knoxville

NASHVILLE

Clingmans Dome 6,643 ft.

Great Smoky Mountains

Shelbyville

Tennessee River

NORTH CAROLINA

Memphis

MISSISSIPPI

ALABAMA

Chattanooga

GEORGIA

Endangered species: Spruce-fir moss spider. This tiny tarantula (1/10") lives only on moss-covered boulders in old-growth forests.

The Sunsphere Tower at Knoxville's 1982 World's Fair symbolized the fair's theme, "Energy Turns the World."

State flower: Iris

State wildflower: The passionflower was the original state flower. In 1933, it was changed to the state wildflower.

Tennessee walking horses are raised near Shelbyville and prized for their smooth gait.

Tennessee
Volunteer State

16th state • Statehood: June 1, 1796 • Population: 5,430,621 • Area: 42,146 square miles

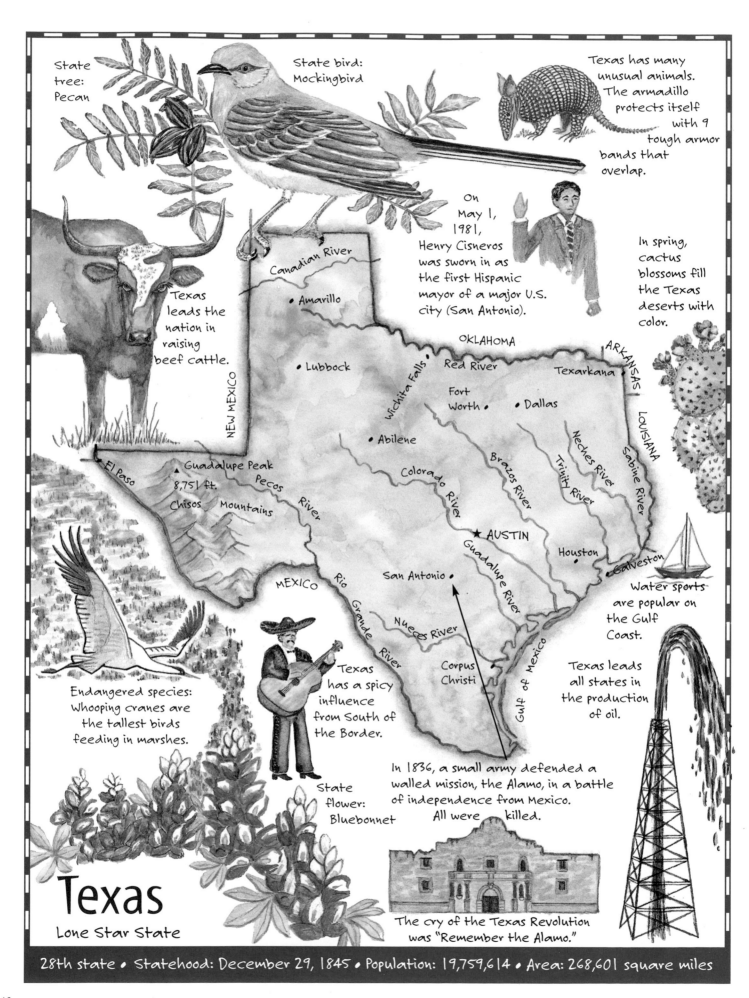

State tree: Pecan

State bird: Mockingbird

Texas has many unusual animals. The armadillo protects itself with 9 tough armor bands that overlap.

On May 1, 1981, Henry Cisneros was sworn in as the first Hispanic mayor of a major U.S. city (San Antonio).

In spring, cactus blossoms fill the Texas deserts with color.

Texas leads the nation in raising beef cattle.

Canadian River

• Amarillo

• Lubbock

NEW MEXICO

OKLAHOMA

ARKANSAS

Red River

Wichita Falls •

Fort Worth •

• Texarkana

• Dallas

LOUISIANA

• Abilene

Neches River

Sabine River

El Paso

▲ Guadalupe Peak 8,751 ft.

Pecos River

Colorado River

Brazos River

Trinity River

Chisos Mountains

★ AUSTIN

Houston •

Galveston

MEXICO

Rio Grande River

San Antonio •

Guadalupe River

Nueces River

Water sports are popular on the Gulf Coast.

Gulf of Mexico

Corpus Christi

Texas leads all states in the production of oil.

Endangered species: Whooping cranes are the tallest birds feeding in marshes.

Texas has a spicy influence from South of the Border.

State flower: Bluebonnet

In 1836, a small army defended a walled mission, the Alamo, in a battle of independence from Mexico. All were killed.

Texas
Lone Star State

The cry of the Texas Revolution was "Remember the Alamo."

28th state • Statehood: December 29, 1845 • Population: 19,759,614 • Area: 268,601 square miles

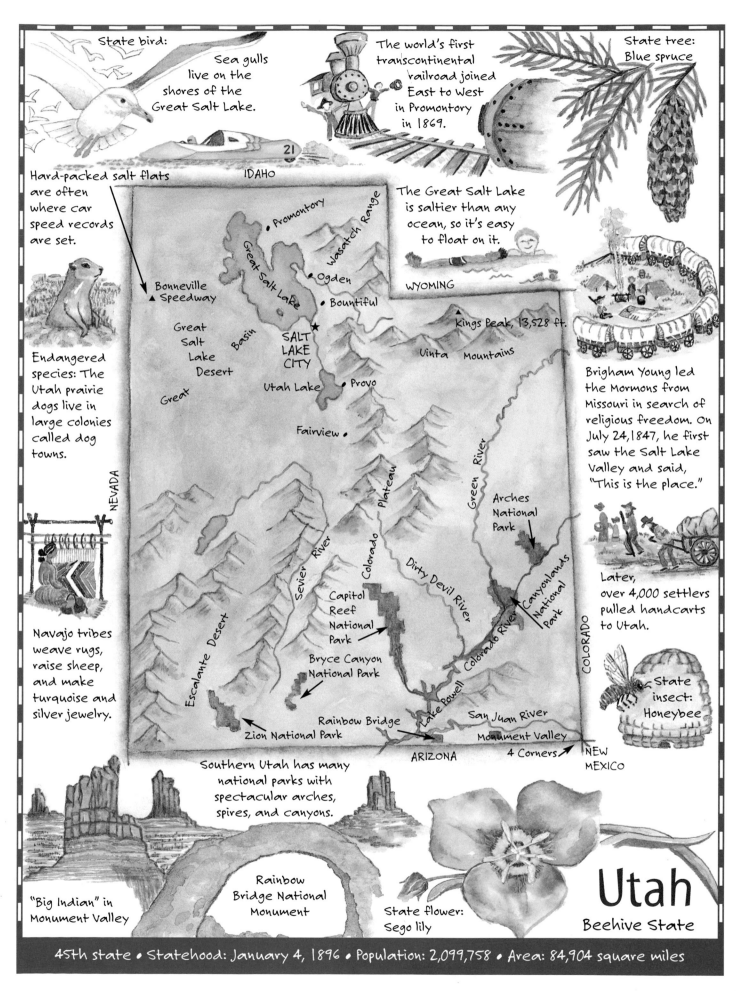

State bird: Sea gulls live on the shores of the Great Salt Lake.

The world's first transcontinental railroad joined East to West in Promontory in 1869.

State tree: Blue spruce

Hard-packed salt flats are often where car speed records are set.

The Great Salt Lake is saltier than any ocean, so it's easy to float on it.

Endangered species: The Utah prairie dogs live in large colonies called dog towns.

Brigham Young led the Mormons from Missouri in search of religious freedom. On July 24, 1847, he first saw the Salt Lake Valley and said, "This is the place."

Navajo tribes weave rugs, raise sheep, and make turquoise and silver jewelry.

Later, over 4,000 settlers pulled handcarts to Utah.

State insect: Honeybee

IDAHO

WYOMING

NEVADA

COLORADO

ARIZONA

NEW MEXICO

Promontory

Wasatch Range

Great Salt Lake

Ogden

Bountiful

Bonneville Speedway

Great Salt Lake Desert

Basin

SALT LAKE CITY

Kings Peak, 13,528 ft.

Uinta Mountains

Great

Utah Lake

Provo

Fairview

Green River

Arches National Park

Plateau

Colorado

Dirty Devil River

Canyonlands National Park

Sevier River

Capitol Reef National Park

Bryce Canyon National Park

Escalante Desert

Zion National Park

Rainbow Bridge

Lake Powell

Colorado River

San Juan River

Monument Valley

4 Corners

"Big Indian" in Monument Valley

Rainbow Bridge National Monument

Southern Utah has many national parks with spectacular arches, spires, and canyons.

State flower: Sego lily

Utah
Beehive State

45th state • Statehood: January 4, 1896 • Population: 2,099,758 • Area: 84,904 square miles

Marble and granite are mined in Vermont.

State insect: Honeybee

Both cross-country and downhill skiing are popular in the Vermont mountains.

Ethan Allen led Vermont's Green Mountain Boys in the American Revolution. His statue, made of Vermont marble, is in Washington, D.C.

CANADA

Lake Champlain

Endangered species: Jesup's milk-vetch grows in limestone riverbanks.

• Burlington

▲ Mt. Mansfield 4,393 ft.

Winooski River

MONTPELIER

• St. Johnsbury

Maple trees are tapped in late winter to collect maple syrup.

NEW YORK

Much electronic equipment is made in Vermont.

• Middlebury

• Barre has the largest granite quarries in the U.S.A.

Otter Creek

Green Mountains

White River

Connecticut River

State bird: Hermit thrush

State tree: Sugar maple

Woodstock •

• Rutland

Springfield •

NEW HAMPSHIRE

State flower: Red clover

Bennington •

Brattleboro •

MASSACHUSETTS

Vermont was the first state after the original 13 colonies to join the union.

Vermont
Green Mountain State

The most rural state in the nation.

Vermont citizens come together each March for town meetings to decide local matters. It's a state holiday.

14th state • Statehood: March 4, 1791 • Population: 590,883 • Area: 9,615 square miles

State bird: Cardinal (This picture shows a female.)

Mount Vernon was George Washington's home.

Eight presidents came from Virginia, more than from any other state: Washington, Jefferson, Madison, Monroe, William Henry Harrison, Tyler, Taylor, and Wilson.

Water carved away soft rock, leaving the Natural Bridge.

The Pentagon is five sided.

It is one of the largest office buildings in the world and holds U.S. government agencies.

Endangered species: The northern flying squirrel can glide over 150 feet through the air.

State tree and state flower: Flowering dogwood

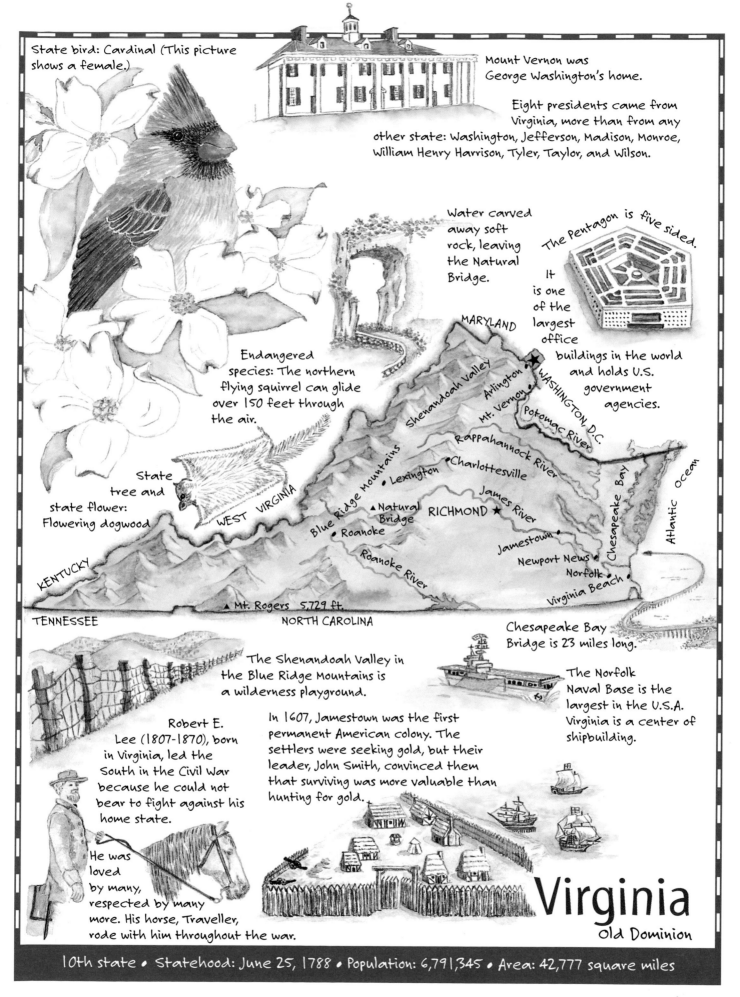

MARYLAND

Shenandoah Valley

Arlington

Mt. Vernon

WASHINGTON, D.C.

Potomac River

Rappahannock River

Charlottesville

Lexington

Blue Ridge Mountains

WEST VIRGINIA

Natural Bridge

RICHMOND ★

James River

Roanoke

Jamestown

Newport News

Norfolk

Chesapeake Bay

Atlantic Ocean

Virginia Beach

Roanoke River

KENTUCKY

▲ Mt. Rogers 5,729 ft.

TENNESSEE

NORTH CAROLINA

Chesapeake Bay Bridge is 23 miles long.

The Shenandoah Valley in the Blue Ridge Mountains is a wilderness playground.

The Norfolk Naval Base is the largest in the U.S.A. Virginia is a center of shipbuilding.

Robert E. Lee (1807-1870), born in Virginia, led the South in the Civil War because he could not bear to fight against his home state.

He was loved by many, respected by many more. His horse, Traveller, rode with him throughout the war.

In 1607, Jamestown was the first permanent American colony. The settlers were seeking gold, but their leader, John Smith, convinced them that surviving was more valuable than hunting for gold.

Virginia
Old Dominion

10th state • Statehood: June 25, 1788 • Population: 6,791,345 • Area: 42,777 square miles

Washington grows more apples than anywhere else in the U.S.A.

Tacoma has the world's tallest totem pole, 105 feet high. Many Pacific Northwest tribes have family or clan emblems on their poles.

Endangered species: Olive ridley sea turtles mate in the Pacific Ocean.

State flower: Coast rhododendron loves the rain-forest climate of western Washington.

CANADA

San Juan Islands

Strait of Juan de Fuca

Bellingham

Skagit River

Puget Sound

Olympic Mountains

Cascade Mountains

Wenatchee Mountains

Lake Chelan

Okanogan River

Rocky Mountains

Pend Oreille River

Grand Coulee Dam

Spokane River

Spokane

IDAHO

Pacific Ocean

Seattle

Tacoma

Wenatchee

Wenatchee River

Columbia River

Columbia Plateau

★OLYMPIA

Centralia

Mt. Rainer 14,410 ft.

Yakima

Yakima River

Snake River

Walla Walla

The Space Needle, a tower in Seattle, is 607 feet high. An elevator takes people to see the view from the top.

Mt. St. Helens erupted May 18, 1980, spitting ashes around the world.

Vancouver

Columbia River

OREGON

Sockeye and chinook salmon are born in freshwater rivers, swim to the ocean, and return to their birthplace to spawn.

State tree: Western hemlock and other evergreens cover half the state.

The only state named after a president

State bird: Goldfinch. These "wild canaries" are found coast to coast.

Washington
Evergreen State

42nd state • Statehood: November 11, 1889 • Population: 5,689,263 • Area: 71,302 square miles

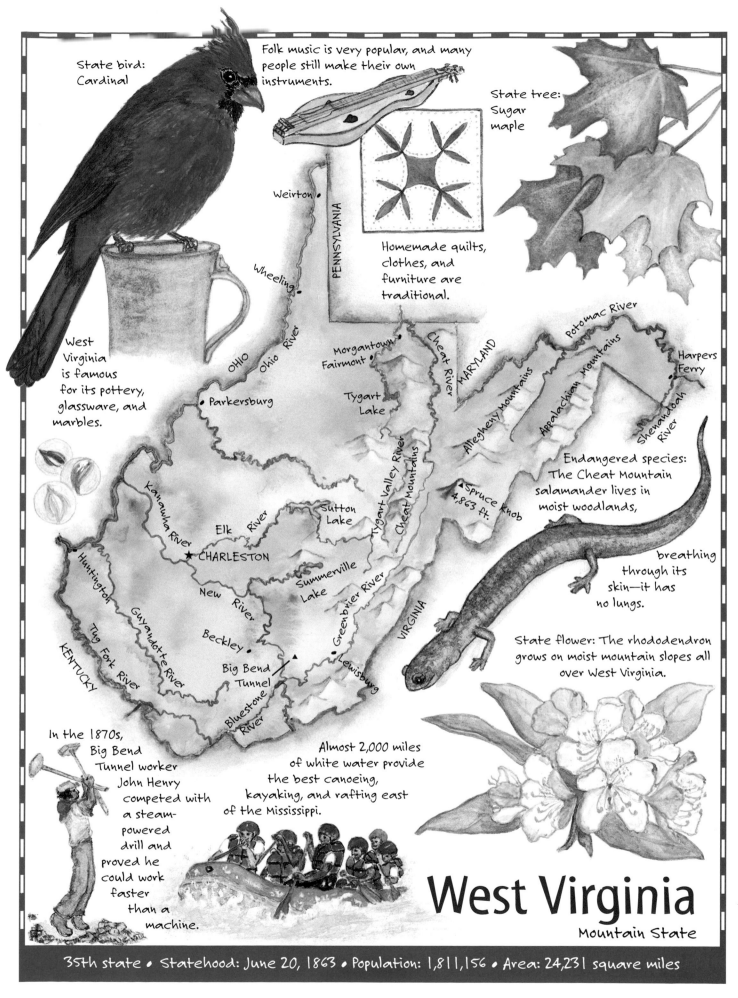

State bird: Cardinal

Folk music is very popular, and many people still make their own instruments.

State tree: Sugar maple

Homemade quilts, clothes, and furniture are traditional.

West Virginia is famous for its pottery, glassware, and marbles.

Weirton

PENNSYLVANIA

Wheeling

OHIO

Ohio River

Morgantown
Fairmont

Cheat River

MARYLAND

Potomac River

Harpers Ferry

Parkersburg

Tygart Lake

Allegheny Mountains

Appalachian Mountains

Shenandoah River

Kanawha River

Elk River

Sutton Lake

Tygart Valley River

Cheat Mountains

▲Spruce Knob 4,863 ft.

Endangered species: The Cheat Mountain salamander lives in moist woodlands,

★ CHARLESTON

Huntington

Guyandotte River

Summerville Lake

Greenbrier River

VIRGINIA

breathing through its skin—it has no lungs.

New River

Tug Fork River

Beckley

Big Bend Tunnel

Lewisburg

State flower: The rhododendron grows on moist mountain slopes all over West Virginia.

KENTUCKY

Bluestone River

In the 1870s, Big Bend Tunnel worker John Henry competed with a steam-powered drill and proved he could work faster than a machine.

Almost 2,000 miles of white water provide the best canoeing, kayaking, and rafting east of the Mississippi.

West Virginia
Mountain State

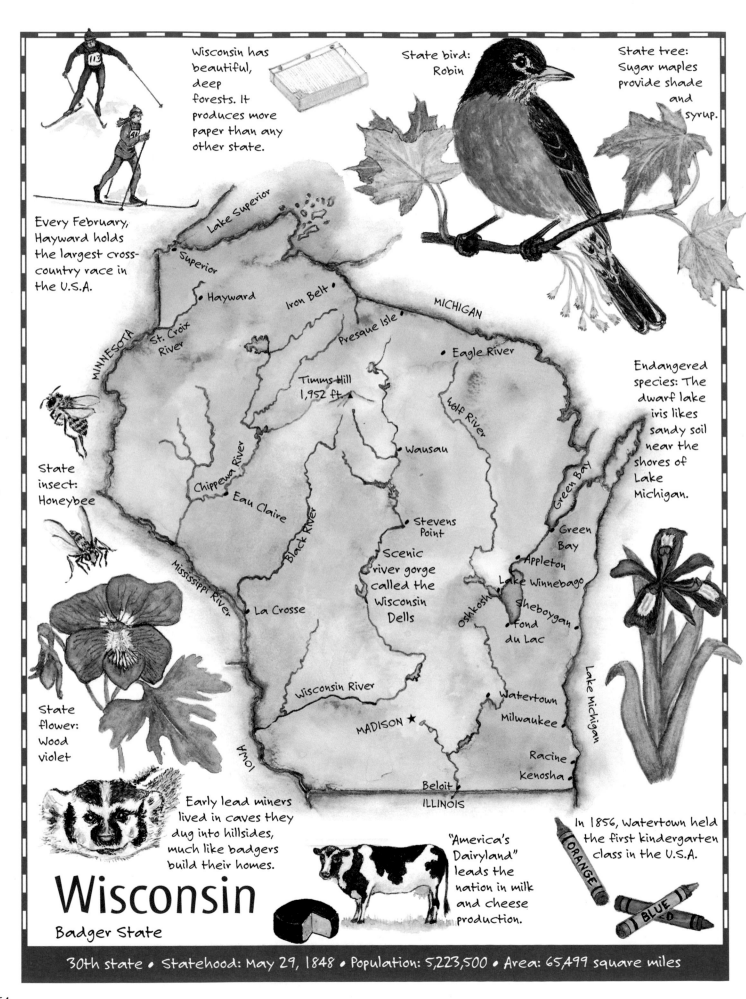

Wisconsin has beautiful, deep forests. It produces more paper than any other state.

State bird: Robin

State tree: Sugar maples provide shade and syrup.

Every February, Hayward holds the largest cross-country race in the U.S.A.

Endangered species: The dwarf lake iris likes sandy soil near the shores of Lake Michigan.

State insect: Honeybee

State flower: Wood violet

Early lead miners lived in caves they dug into hillsides, much like badgers build their homes.

"America's Dairyland" leads the nation in milk and cheese production.

In 1856, Watertown held the first kindergarten class in the U.S.A.

ORANGE
BLUE

Wisconsin
Badger State

MINNESOTA
Lake Superior
Superior
Hayward
Iron Belt
MICHIGAN
St. Croix River
Presque Isle
Eagle River
Timms Hill 1,952 ft.
Wolf River
Wausau
Chippewa River
Eau Claire
Stevens Point
Green Bay
Green Bay
Appleton
Lake Winnebago
Oshkosh
Sheboygan
Fond du Lac
Black River
Mississippi River
La Crosse
Scenic river gorge called the Wisconsin Dells
Wisconsin River
MADISON ★
Watertown
Milwaukee
Lake Michigan
Racine
Kenosha
Beloit
ILLINOIS
IOWA

30th state • Statehood: May 29, 1848 • Population: 5,223,500 • Area: 65,499 square miles

54

State bird: Meadowlark

State tree: Cottonwood

In 1872, before Wyoming was a state, Yellowstone became the first national park.

In 1869, Wyoming women were the first to vote. Women in other states had to wait 50 years.

Sheep and cattle graze on more than half the state.

MONTANA

Old Faithful Geyser

Yellowstone National Park

Shoshone National Forest

Shoshone River

Sheridan

Bighorn Mountains

Powder River

Gillette

Belle Fourche River

Devils Tower

Black Hills

SOUTH DAKOTA

Yellowstone Lake is the largest high-altitude lake in the U.S.A. It is usually frozen over half the year.

Bighorn River

Grand Tetons

Jackson Lake

Snake River

Kelly Jackson

Thermopolis

Bridger Mountains

Devils Tower is the core of an ancient volcano and sacred to many Indian tribes. In 1906, it became the first national monument.

Gannett Peak 13,804 ft.

Rocky Mountains

Wind River

Riverton

North Platte River

Casper

NEBRASKA

In 1891, Shoshone National Forest became the first national forest.

Salt River Range

Continental Divide

Sweetwater River

Laramie

Green River

Great Divide Basin water doesn't flow east or west it stays.

Rawlins

North Platte River

Laramie River

Laramie Mountains

IDAHO

UTAH

Green River

Rock Springs

Laramie

Flaming Gorge Reservoir

CHEYENNE

COLORADO

State flower: Indian paintbrush

Endangered species: The Wyoming toad still lives in a few marshes near the Laramie River. It is one of the rarest amphibians in the world.

Frontier Days are celebrations of Wyoming's history, full of rodeos and Native American ceremonies.

Wyoming
Equality State

44th state • Statehood: July 10, 1890 • Population: 480,907 • Area: 97,818 square miles

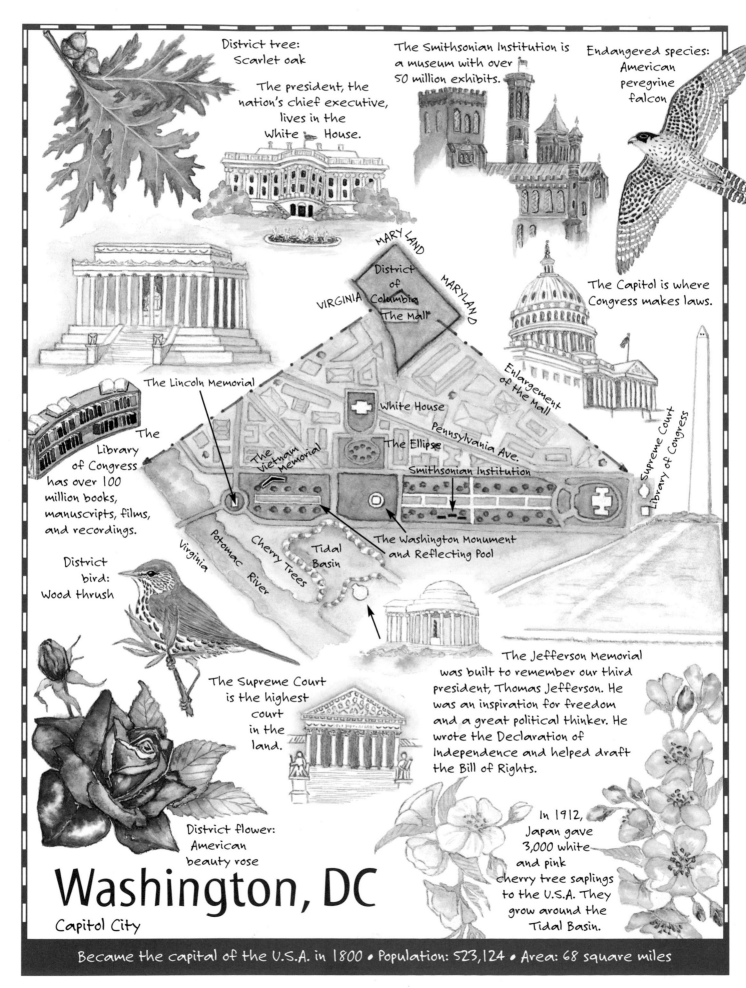

District tree: Scarlet oak

The president, the nation's chief executive, lives in the White House.

The Smithsonian Institution is a museum with over 50 million exhibits.

Endangered species: American peregrine falcon

MARYLAND

District of Columbia

VIRGINIA

MARYLAND

The Mall

The Capitol is where Congress makes laws.

The Lincoln Memorial

The Library of Congress has over 100 million books, manuscripts, films, and recordings.

Enlargement of the Mall

White House

Pennsylvania Ave.

The Ellipse

Smithsonian Institution

The Vietnam Memorial

Supreme Court

Library of Congress

Potomac River

Cherry Trees

Tidal Basin

The Washington Monument and Reflecting Pool

District bird: Wood thrush

Virginia

The Supreme Court is the highest court in the land.

The Jefferson Memorial was built to remember our third president, Thomas Jefferson. He was an inspiration for freedom and a great political thinker. He wrote the Declaration of Independence and helped draft the Bill of Rights.

District flower: American beauty rose

In 1912, Japan gave 3,000 white and pink cherry tree saplings to the U.S.A. They grow around the Tidal Basin.

Washington, DC

Capitol City

Became the capital of the U.S.A. in 1800 • Population: 523,124 • Area: 68 square miles

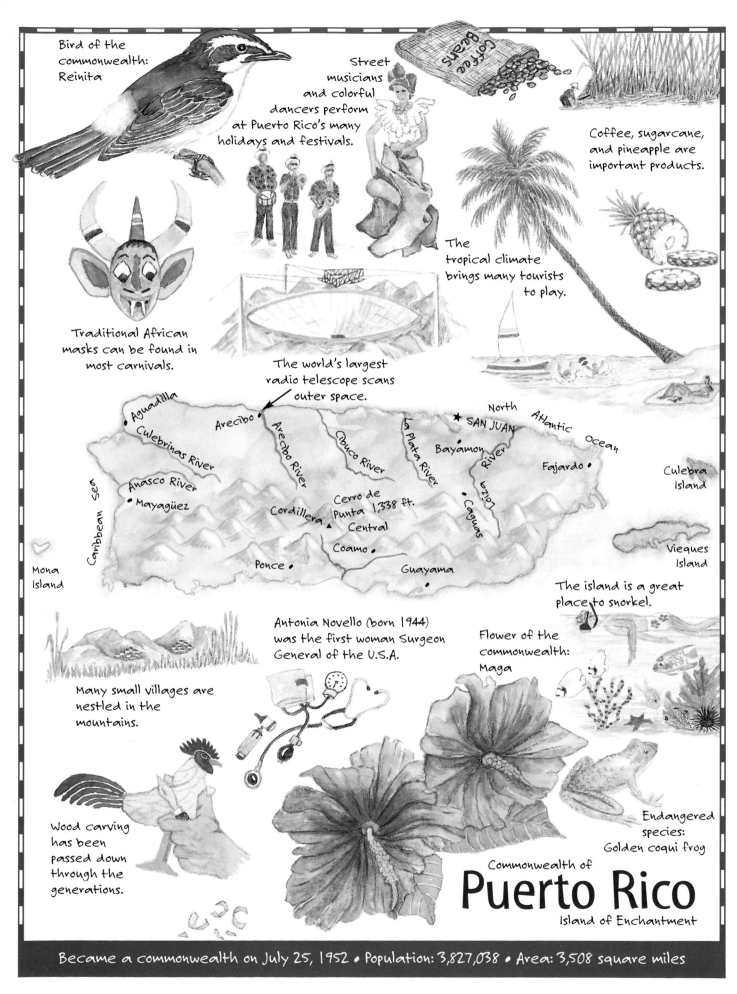

Bird of the commonwealth: Reinita

Street musicians and colorful dancers perform at Puerto Rico's many holidays and festivals.

Coffee beans

Coffee, sugarcane, and pineapple are important products.

Traditional African masks can be found in most carnivals.

The tropical climate brings many tourists to play.

The world's largest radio telescope scans outer space.

North Atlantic Ocean

Aguadilla

Arecibo

★ SAN JUAN

Bayamon

Culebrinas River

Arecibo River

Cibuco River

La Plata River

Loiza River

Fajardo

Culebra Island

Anasco River

Mayagüez

Caribbean Sea

Cerro de Punta 1,338 ft.

Cordillera Central

Caguas

Vieques Island

Coamo

Mona Island

Ponce

Guayama

The island is a great place to snorkel.

Many small villages are nestled in the mountains.

Antonia Novello (born 1944) was the first woman Surgeon General of the U.S.A.

Flower of the commonwealth: Maga

Wood carving has been passed down through the generations.

Endangered species: Golden coqui frog

Commonwealth of
Puerto Rico
Island of Enchantment

Became a commonwealth on July 25, 1952 • Population: 3,827,038 • Area: 3,508 square miles

"Old Glory," The United States of America

Alabama

Alaska

Connecticut

Delaware

Illinois

Indiana

Iowa

Kansas

Massachusetts

Michigan

Minnesota

Mississippi

New Hampshire

New Jersey

New Mexico

New York

Oregon

Pennsylvania

Rhode Island

South Carolina

Vermont

Virginia

Washington

West Virginia

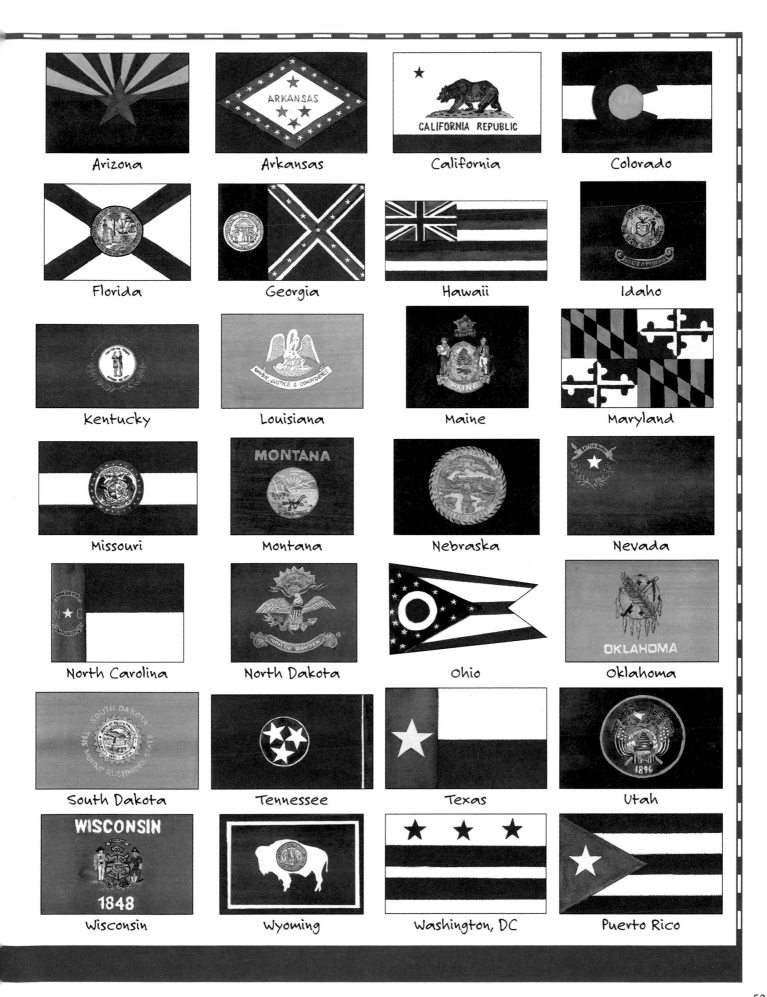

Arizona

Arkansas

California

Colorado

Florida

Georgia

Hawaii

Idaho

Kentucky

Louisiana

Maine

Maryland

Missouri

Montana

Nebraska

Nevada

North Carolina

North Dakota

Ohio

Oklahoma

South Dakota

Tennessee

Texas

Utah

Wisconsin

Wyoming

Washington, DC

Puerto Rico

I N D E X

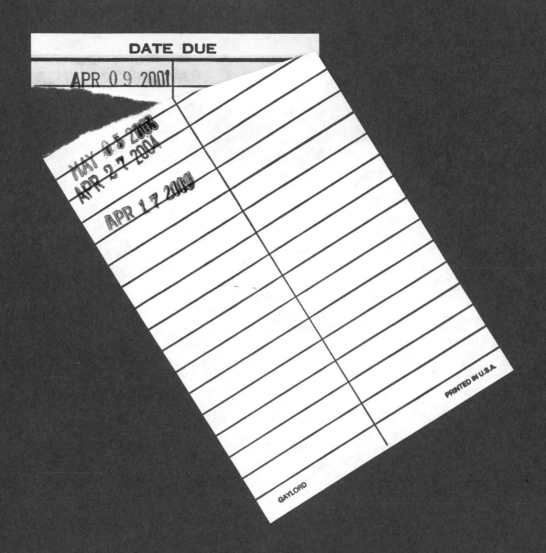